What are people saying about
A Pawn's Journey

"Elliott Neff has produced a compelling narrative that unfolds the mindset and disciplines necessary to excel in life. I found myself nodding in agreement as Elliott highlighted the shared attitudes common among those driven to live a life of meaning."

Jason Anspach,
#1 bestselling author and co-creator of *Galaxy's Edge*

"A must-read for parents who are serious about their children's success in school, college, and life."

Verne Harnish,
Founder Entrepreneurs' Organization (EO) and author of *Scaling Up (Rockefeller Habits 2.0)*

"Elliott Neff is a masterful storyteller in this moving tale. Parents, share this story with your children!"

Orrin C. Hudson,
Executive Director, Be Someone, Inc

"A Pawn's Journey is an engaging and emotional quest about discovering our natural gifts. This uplifting story will get you energized to chase your dreams!"

Mary Miller,
co-creator of The Dream Manager, CEO JANCOA, Speaker & Author

I

"I read this page-turner straight through! Couldn't put it down! The story will inspire students and parents, and everyone who is or has a high schooler needs to read it. Elliott Neff knows from his experience as a chess master the principles that will transform the lives of students, and when you finish reading, you will too. And you don't need to know anything about chess to understand and enjoy the book."

Dr. Joseph Castleberry,
President, Northwest University and
author of *Forty Days of Christmas*

"In this engaging story, young April learns life lessons while learning the game of chess. Author Elliott Neff demonstrates his life-master chess skills, his master teaching abilities, and great insights on navigating the challenges of life."

Dr. Albert Erisman,
Author of *The Accidental Executive: Lessons on Business, Faith,* and *Calling from the life of Joseph*; Boeing executive (retired)

"Anyone hoping to prepare their children for success should read this inspiring page-turner by Elliott Neff! Readers will learn how all children can discover their unique abilities and flourish as they are captivated by April's journey of self-discovery through chess."

Hao Lam,
CEO of Best in Class Education Center
and author of *From Bad to Worse to Best in Class: A Refugee's Success Story*

"Every chess coach and every chess parent – indeed every coach of any kind and every parent and every teacher – should read Elliott Neff's inspiring words on the power of imagination, intention, and inclusion to create a vibrant and positive life. Blending narration and didacticism, *A Pawn's Journey* let's see through the imaginative eyes of adults and children who won't settle for anything less than the best effort, no matter what the obstacles."

Dr. Mark Trevor Smith,
English Emeritus, Missouri State University

"It can be those early life lessons that become the foundation for one's future. Those life lessons shape family, career, leaders... and impact communities – when they are the right life lessons, it's all for good. *A Pawn's Journey* builds into our future leaders, eternal values & principles."

Jeff R. Rogers,
Chairman of OneAccord and
founder of www.KIROS.org

"Neff captures the spirit of our times- the search for justice, humanity, and excellence- within the metaphor of his area of expertise- Chess. A book that will inspire kids of all ages to pursue their passions in the pursuit of a rewarding and giving life."

Romi Mahajan,
CEO KKM Group, Director Blueprint,
Author, Marketer, Activist

"Elliott Neff's charming allegory is a must-read. Elliott uses the game of chess to release untapped potential in a diverse set of characters. He challenges stereotypes, evoking empathy and compassion in the reader. No matter the life-stage or circumstance, readers are motivated to implement meaningful thinking tools to achieve bold goals. This book will help release people's inner potential as they rediscover their passion for positively impacting youth."

Catherine Crosslin,
CEO Instar Performance, elevating thinking and
releasing potential in people around the world

"*A Pawn's Journey* follows the main character, April, from learning the rules of chess to a valued high school chess team member. Readers will cheer as April uses life lessons from chess at the state championship and on a life-changing STEM project, supported by a colorful cast of teammates, family members, and a chess master."

Dr. Alexey Root,
author of *Children and Chess: A Guide for Educators*

"This engaging story perfectly summarizes why today's youth need STEM and chess in their lives! *A Pawn's Journey* is so engaging; I couldn't stop reading it!. This will be the book your children and students can't put down, mainly because so many can relate to this journey."

Denise "Cookie" Bouldin,
Seattle Police Detective and founder of the
Detective Cookie Urban Youth Chess Club

"The ancient game of chess made accessible for young people today through a compelling story – hopefully this tale will inspire the next generation of chess champions!"

Matt Watrous,
Director of Government Relations,
Midwest Region, Boys & Girls Clubs of America

"This is a must-read book for success seekers. A terrific distillation of the essential fundamental skills needed in the game of life."

Mike Sayenko,
CEO, Sayenko Design

"*A Pawn's Journey* held me captive from the opening paragraph to the very end and capped off a fantastic Saturday before Easter (I completed the book in nearly one sitting)! I found myself not only grateful for the meaning of tomorrow's Holiday celebration but for Mr. Neff's capture of a story within a story and one that reminded me warmly of my own life and Mr. Johnson, my seventh-grade math teacher. I am so grateful for his introduction of chess to a group of underserved, inner city youth from a poor city and for the impact it had for the Black Knights and our many first-place finishes not only in chess tournaments but in life! Mr. Neff, thanks for the memories!"

Calvin L. Lyons,
President & CEO,
Boys & Girls Clubs of Metro Los Angeles

"A captivating, relatable story that invites discovery of unique abilities - a practical guide to life-transforming values through the catalyst of chess."

Raphael Neff,
CEO, ChessHouse.com

"Future generations will realize the power of human potential through Elliott's masterful utilization of chess and its boundless capabilities."

J.K. Egerton,
CEO & Founder, Business on the Board

"This book has exactly what you need to know about the basic building blocks of life skills using chess. It articulates well key perspectives and principles of life. I highly recommend this book for every family."

Benjamin Mukumbya,
Student of SOM Chess Academy in Uganda

"What can I possibly say that could communicate my assessment of Elliott Neff and his Chess Magic? His vision, enthusiasm, success, and integrity have developed a mindset and an organization that is truly sensational. Whoever is exposed to his concepts and beliefs will be on a journey of success and validation of the human spirit."

John W Meisenbach,
Chairman MCM

"This charming, thoughtful, metaphor-rich journey of self-discovery is a must-read for anyone seeking to find the genius within themselves."

Siva Sankrithi,
Teacher and CEO of WIISER

"*A Pawn's Journey* is a delightful story which imparts wisdom on many levels. The attentive reader is inspired and learns what it takes to develop a more noble character."

David Giannini,
CFP, Private Asset Management

"Elliott Neff wrote a "feel good" book that contains a roadmap to help you in your life. A bonus is that he shows the game of chess to be exciting and dramatic. Very nice!"

Gary Sirak,
author of *The American Dream Revisited*

"Elliott Neff has made a difference for thousands of kids through his popular chess education programs. Now, through *A Pawn's Journey*, he shares the powerful story that he has observed time and again in the lives he has touched - a story of purpose, determination, and human excellence."

Hans Zeiger,
Washington State Senator

A PAWN'S JOURNEY

TRANSFORMING LIVES
ONE MOVE AT A TIME

ELLIOTT NEFF

Made for Success
PUBLISHING

PUBLISHED BY MADE FOR SUCCESS PUBLISHING,
a division of Made for Success, Inc., Seattle, Washington.

If you are seeking to purchase this book in quantity for sales
promotion or corporate use, please contact Made for Success at
425-657-0300 or email Sales@MadeforSuccess.net. Your local
bookstore can also help you with discounted bulk purchase options.

Library of Congress Cataloging-in-Publication data

Neff, Elliott
A Pawn's Journey: Transforming Lives One Move at a Time

ISBN: 978-1-64146-316-4 (PBK)
ISBN: 978-1-64146-317-1 (EBOOK)
LCCN: 2018945961

Printed in the United States of America

DEDICATION

To the love of my life, Camilla, who believes in my abilities more than I do myself, and sacrificed so much by encouraging me to take the time to write this book. Without your encouragement and belief, I would not be who I am today, and this book would not be here.

FOREWORD

Several years ago, I had just wrapped up a speaking engagement in Chapel Hill, N.C., when a member of the audience approached me and said, "I think I have a good story for you."

As a former senior writer at *Sports Illustrated*, I've heard that a lot over the years, but I've been trained to listen to every idea. The gentleman told me that he'd recently received a newsletter that included an article about a young girl, Phiona Mutesi, who grew up in a Ugandan slum called Katwe. Phiona had dropped out of school after her father died. She could neither read nor write, and she was essentially homeless. Phiona was selling maize in the slum when one day she crossed paths with a Ugandan missionary named Robert Katende, who offered to teach her to play chess, a game so foreign to her that there is no word for it in her native language. Four years later, Phiona was crowned an international chess champion.

After reading the item in the newsletter, I arranged a meeting with Rodney Suddith, the president of Sports Outreach Institute, the American organization that sponsors Katende's mission. Suddith had written the story about Phiona, and he'd spent some time with her, so I asked him to share whatever he could about her journey. He detailed Phiona's remarkable personal transformation through Katende's mentorship in chess and then, in conclusion,

Suddith shared a piece of advice that has stuck with me ever since. "If you decide to write this story, don't do it for Phiona," he said. "Do it for all of the other Phionas."

I must admit that at the time I wasn't exactly sure what Suddith meant. It wasn't until I traveled to Katwe later that year to meet Katende, Phiona and the rest of the children in the Katwe chess program that it began to dawn on me. I was starting to meet some of the other Phionas. A few years later, Phiona visited the United States for the first time, and she was invited into my son's third grade class to teach chess to 20 students, 20 other Phionas, who were so inspired that they kept asking to play chess for weeks and months after that. Phiona's appearance eventually sparked the creation of a chess club at the school that now mentors 250 other Phionas in chess each year. Our book, *The Queen of Katwe*, is now published in a dozen languages and the Disney movie it spawned has encouraged countless other Phionas. I regularly receive emails from these other Phionas all over the world, both girls and boys, who have been motivated by the story to overcome the myriad of obstacles in their lives and chase dreams they once thought unattainable.

Phiona's message is powerful. Katende's mission is powerful. The author of this book, Elliott Neff, shares their passion. Elliott has worked closely alongside Robert Katende and Phiona Mutesi. Nobody better understands the potential impact of chess in transforming young people and now Elliott, too, is reaching out to all of the other Phionas through this compelling book.

After reading *A Pawn's Journey*, I can't help but think that April is yet another one of those Phionas and that she has a good story for you.

Tim Crothers

PREFACE

"Thank you for teaching our son this season. He's done very well! But that's not why we invited you to dinner."

The parents of one of my students were speaking, as we were sitting in an upscale restaurant in downtown Seattle. Their statement caught my attention, and I listened even more carefully.

They went on to share with me how that over the prior season of my coaching their son in the game of chess they had observed their son's grades in school improve to where he was now top in his class. They said that he was now focusing on his homework daily, completing it accurately and quickly, without their pressuring him to do it. He had also grown more considerate and respectful of others.

They finished by saying, "He just doesn't give up easily like he used to. We've seen his character develop in a good way - and we believe it's in large part because of your mentorship while you've been coaching him in chess. We're happy he's done well in chess competitions - but these other things are what really matters to us and why we are so very grateful for your coaching him! Thank-you again!"

I was at a loss for what to say and could simply manage, "Thank-you for sharing this, it's been a joy to work with him this year."

That dinner meeting and several others were a catalyst leading to my dedicating my life to see these outcomes and benefits made available to as many students as possible.

In January of 2014, I had the privilege of meeting Robert Katende and Phiona Mutesi who featured in the book *The Queen of Katwe* (and later on Disney's *Queen of Katwe* movie based on that book). Visiting the work Robert started in the slums of Uganda, and seeing the progress of his SOM Chess Academy, further brought home to me that the positive outcomes of developing life skills through chess are indeed globally applicable.

Over time, many people would ask me, "What do you mean when you say *Life Skills hrough Chess?*" Each time I would think of the many students' lives I had seen transformed, and launch into one or another story to explain what I meant. Eventually, I thought, *maybe I should write a book to answer the question so people can enjoy and understand more fully how chess can be an amazing vehicle for positive change.*

A Pawn's Journey is that idea turned into reality.

The book you hold was inspired by many students. I hope April's story inspires you.

CHAPTER 1

CATHY WAS WALKING past the lockers as she headed towards the high school staff workroom when something caught her attention. She noticed one girl close her locker and just stand there for a bit. When the girl started to move away, Cathy thought she heard her sigh. Cathy slowed down and tapped her on the shoulder. "Excuse me; my name is Cathy. What's yours?" As the girl turned around, Cathy noted that she was dressed simply, though tastefully. Cathy thought she noticed sadness in April's eyes – eyes that in color nearly matched her black, shoulder-length, and rather curly, hair. "I'm April," the girl said.

Cathy spoke in a gentle voice, "Is something wrong?" April struggled to hold back her tears.

Cathy noticed, and not waiting for an answer, put her hand gently on April's arm as she said, "Here, why don't we go into the teachers' lounge for a few minutes."

Finding a quiet corner of the lounge, they sat down. Cathy said, "I'm sorry for interrupting you, but I can tell there's something wrong. Do you mind sharing it with me?"

Although hesitant at first, April slowly opened up to Cathy.

She explained how her dad's commute was nearly an hour to work at a toy manufacturing and distribution company and that he left early and often worked late while trying to advance in the company. She had a 9-year-old brother Max, as well as a 17-year-old brother Michael. Michael seemed to be able to do everything – he excelled in school, won a scholarship to college, played a key role on the baseball team, and all in addition to being heavily involved in the Robotics Club. April's mom Sara was a dedicated school teacher and was so busy that she frequently asked April to watch Max after school as well as on weekends.

April went on to explain how she had overheard her parents talking about the difficulties of saving enough for college and how helpful it was that Michael was winning scholarships that would likely pay for his college tuition.

April tried to put into words her longing for something when she heard them talk about Michael in such glowing terms – the feeling of wanting her parents, especially her Dad, to be proud of her. Yes, her parents were loving and kind, but she had the feeling that she was not living up to their expectations. While her grades in school were never all that bad, neither were they outstanding like Michael's. Her parents never said it, but she compared herself to her older brother – and had a tendency to just get along.

Overhearing her parents' conversation had got April thinking of what she could do – and she finally decided she would try out for the soccer team. She thought that perhaps she could get on the team and just maybe earn a scholarship there. She had started playing soccer with Max when looking after him on Saturdays, working to improve her ability to kick the ball, and started dreaming of winning a scholarship. But when it came to tryouts for the team, she found her hopes quickly crushed. Not only did she not make it onto the team, the coach, though kind, made it quite clear that he didn't see a future in soccer for her.

Thinking of this failure trying out for the soccer team and feeling as if she couldn't do anything well had led to the sigh that Cathy noticed.

April struggled to blink back tears as she finished her story.

Cathy listened quietly, and when April finished, she put her arm around April's shoulders, giving her a gentle hug, thinking for a minute.

"April," Cathy finally said, "I want you to know something. It seems to me that many people see the abilities that others have, just as you see the abilities in Michael – yet often have difficulty recognizing their own incredible abilities. I believe that you too have amazing abilities. It's a matter of discovering them, and in many cases, I believe that it's mostly a matter of developing a number of mindsets or life skills that unlock an individual's unique abilities." Cathy paused for a few moments to let her words sink in, then continued, "April, I have an idea – would you like to join me on a short journey to learn about your own unique abilities? Who knows, perhaps you may discover some things along the way that will change you…" Cathy stopped mid-sentence and stood up abruptly.

"What kinds of things do you mean?" April asked, her interest growing the more Cathy talked, but unsure of what exactly Cathy was alluding to.

"I just realized I'm late for another appointment," Cathy replied. "How about you join me tomorrow afternoon to start this journey? Are you willing to give it a try?"

"Yes, I think so," April said a little hesitantly.

"Excellent," Cathy replied. "Let's meet right after school tomorrow. I have to run. See you tomorrow!"

"Goodbye," April said, and as she walked out, she wondered what journey Cathy had in mind. She was curious, though a little uncertain. Oh well, guess I'll find out tomorrow, she thought, her curiosity for the moment overtaking her hesitancy.

When April arrived home, her mother Sara was busy putting dinner on the table.

"Dad's got another late meeting, so he's not going to make dinner," Sara said, the news more the norm than a surprise to April.

"Any word on the promotion yet?" April asked.

"Not yet," Sara said, "though after all the hard work he's been putting in, seems like it's just a matter of time now."

"When he gets it, do you think Dad will have to be gone as often?" April asked as she started eating.

"Yes, I'm afraid so – likely more often than now," Sara said, then added more to herself than to anyone else, "I sure hope it pays off!" April's mom Sara was a dedicated lifelong teacher, struggling to balance the demands of her large class at school with her family's needs at home. With April's dad Davis working hard for the next promotion, it left Sara to carry much of the needs of her family. While there were times April's mom was pulled in multiple directions, she rarely complained. Instead, she expressed her thankfulness for April's hard-working dad and gratefulness for what they had, as her mother, April's grandmother, had had it much more difficult.

April's grandmother came from a line that could be traced back to those who picked cotton by hand on plantations during the days of slavery. On her dad's side, April's grandparents came from a well-to-do family that traced their ancestry quite proudly all the way back to the first settlers in America.

April knew that her dad loved his family, yet with how much he was gone for work, it seemed to April that when he did attend any of his kids' school events, it was for Michael's competitions. While she had trouble putting it into words, she had the sense that she needed to win at something for her dad to make attending her events a priority.

April went to bed early that night, thinking about her talk with Cathy, and wondering what tomorrow would bring.

CHAPTER 2

CATHY WAS ONE of those people not easily forgotten. When she looked into your eyes, you had the sense that she could see right into your heart, and more, cared about what she saw there. When you spoke with her, she seemed to be listening with every fiber of her body. Yet not all found her entirely comfortable to talk with, as she was a source for creative action that was not necessarily predictable.

Cathy's husband Joe had sold his company two years before, carefully transitioning the leadership to the new owners over the following year. He was now enjoying more time on the golf course – although some people said that he really golfed just to have time to discuss various business ideas and share advice with other business leaders and budding entrepreneurs.

Even though she was not in need of the income, Cathy had been working in the local school district for several years. At first, she had just volunteered but found over time that her ideas were more likely to take root if she had an official position in the district. It was too easy while she was just volunteering for others to dismiss her somewhat unusual approach, which some would even call radical. The superintendent in the district, however, was quite supportive towards Cathy's ideas. He too had an innovative approach and believed that as the world changed rapidly with technology, it was important to rethink education and explore ways to prepare students for a future life radically different than that of their parents and grandparents. When Cathy applied for the role of district enrichment programs coordinator, the superintendent gave his approval readily, though being careful to diplomatically communicate his support for some of her out of the box ideas.

While volunteering, Cathy had already supported a variety of causes, and she thought that there were some activities with significant potential for positively influencing students. With this conviction, Cathy had worked over the last few years to establish a number of clubs. She launched a debate club that was rapidly growing, added coding programs where students loved to build their own computer games while learning foundational coding languages and launched a robotics club that was now district-wide. She spoke constantly about the need for developing additional STEM (Science, Technology, Engineering, Math) related programs, and worked tirelessly to bring others in the district not just to the point of acceptance but also of advocating for these opportunities for students. Cathy did not hesitate to go outside the schools to solicit community funding and support. She was able to establish long-term commitments from sponsors to provide a series of scholarships for the clubs, with the expectation that as the financial incentive of these scholarships grew, so would interest from both students and community.

Once the robotics clubs had gathered momentum, Cathy enlisted the help of a chess master to set up afterschool chess clubs in most of the schools in the district, elementary through high school. She believed that the ancient game would help students develop important life skills and success mindsets, as well as complement her efforts to grow STEM skills. At the very minimum, she felt that learning a game that was perceived as 'complex' or for 'smart kids' would help many students grow in confidence, focus, and decision making – outcomes she believed would help all students.

While pleased with the growth of the STEM-related clubs, Cathy observed something that caused her growing concern – there seemed to be a stigma about girls. Whether robotics, coding, chess, or similar clubs, they all seemed to be heavily male-dominated. Cathy also noticed that there seemed to be a growing perception that the clubs were just for the "smart" or "rich" kids, a notion that appeared to be keeping many students from joining the clubs.

One evening sometime before meeting April, Cathy and Joe were out for dinner at their favorite Italian restaurant. After the appetizers arrived, Joe spoke up. "You're rather quiet tonight. Is something on your mind?"

"Yes," Cathy said slowly, "I've been thinking about what to do about the clubs at school."

"What's wrong with them?" Joe asked. "I thought they were going strong."

"They are indeed going quite well," Cathy said. "It's just that they are going well for the boys, at least some of them – but it seems as if the stronger the clubs become, the fewer the girls that join. On top of that, there seems to be a growing notion that these clubs are really for the well-to-do, smart kids. Exactly the opposite of what I wanted to see! I've wanted to see all the kids benefit, especially those who have not had as much opportunity as others. But at this point, it seems as if the underprivileged, as well as girls, are avoiding the clubs even though we have been able to ensure that there is no barrier in terms of cost."

"Sounds like it's turning into an 'old boys club,'" Joe joked, then added, "But seriously, that does sound like it could be a real challenge."

"Well, I guess it's not quite as bad as it sounds," Cathy said, "but if nothing changes it could become a real issue."

As they ate, Joe and Cathy brainstormed various ways to address the challenge. After considering and discarding several ideas, Joe suddenly spoke up, "That's it! We need a catalyst!"

"A catalyst?" Cathy said quizzically, "What do you mean?"
"Well, you know," Joe said, "when you want to light a fire you need the spark – when you want a chemical reaction you need the catalyst to cause it. Perhaps we just need the right spark. Instead of trying to convince people why girls and underprivileged students should feel welcomed, why not let people simply see it for themselves. Remember when you launched the robotics programs? It took success in just one school to lead to rapid adoption throughout the district. Imagine if you could find one or two students who represent the 'underprivileged' and help them achieve. Their story could be the catalyst for widespread acceptance."

"Hmm," Cathy replied slowly. "One or two succeeding could be seen as the exception to the rule. But if we put a team together and they succeeded, I can see that working. I know just who to invite onto the team!

"There's a new student I heard about who transferred into the district. He has a very unusual story. He's one of the 'differently-abled' students and is a champion-level chess player from Africa attending school in the U.S. thanks to a generous benefactor."

Never one to waste any time before implementing once she had an idea, the following day Cathy approached the principal from the local high school. The high school had the lowest test scores in the district when he came in with high hopes of transforming the school. After two years, he felt he was making progress though slower than he had hoped. Cathy's success with the Robotics club ensured that he at least listened whenever Cathy brought up a new suggestion. It didn't take much convincing for Cathy to get his approval for her plans to start a chess team, and when she added the fact that she had already enlisted the help of a former student from the school who happened to be a strong chess master, her case was won.

Cathy set to work immediately, and it wasn't long before she had put together a small chess team. From low income to high income, from special needs to high-achieving athletic students, Cathy included students representing as much diversity as possible. Cathy was happy with the development of the team, except in one regard – so far she had not had success recruiting any girls to join the group.

Then she met April.

CHAPTER 3

APRIL WOKE UP suddenly, feeling a nervous anticipation and not sure what it meant. She lay still for a few moments wondering. Then she remembered – today was going to be different! She wasn't sure whether to be excited about the possibilities or dread what might happen.

Yesterday's conversation was still puzzling her. What did Cathy mean when she invited April to come with her on what she said was 'a short journey that would change her'? Well, no sense wondering about it. She would find out soon enough.

Shortly after her last class for the day ended, April stopped by her locker for her sweater. As she slowly headed down the hallway towards the exit, she found herself torn between curiosity about the journey Cathy had suggested and hesitancy towards stepping outside her comfort zone into the unknown.

"April!" Cathy said, startling her. She momentarily thought about making an excuse to get out of her commitment, but there was no way out. Cathy was already at her side and easily fell in step with her. Cathy seemed to think that everyone would follow along with her ideas – why wouldn't they? The strength she exuded caused most people to go along unless they had VERY strong reservations and even then, many times those objections were voiced rather quietly if at all.

Cathy saw the hesitation on April's face.

"April," Cathy said, "Remember what you shared with me yesterday? Nothing changes until you take a step beyond what you are familiar with. Today I want you to come with me and meet someone very special."

By now they were nearing the end of the hallway, but rather than turning towards the exit, Cathy turned to the right, heading to the part of the school that April avoided. It was the section where the 'special needs' students came for school – though they weren't called 'special needs.' That was not inclusive enough. Someone had come up with the idea of calling them the 'school projects.' Cathy preferred and rather firmly insisted on saying these kids were the 'differently-abled' students.

"I'll wait for you here," April said, assuming Cathy must have left something in one of the classrooms and was picking it up on the way.

"Actually, April, our journey leads us this way," Cathy said. "In fact, we are almost there."

April's heart sank. This journey was not sounding so fun anymore. *Oh no, not there*, April thought.

It was the classroom that she avoided like the plague. It was bad enough walking past the special needs classrooms, but this one? Here students weren't even able to move about without assistance! They came and went in various types of wheelchairs and other contraptions. April had always assumed that the students who went in there were just not as capable of learning as other students.

Before she could complete her thoughts, Cathy was leading April into the room.

"Hi, I'm Gabe! Shake?"

April stuck out her right hand – then suddenly stopped in bewilderment. The friendly, energetic voice and captivating face held her till she realized that Gabe was sitting in a small wheelchair and quite obviously had no arms!

Gabe smiled even wider at seeing April's confusion, and

repeated, "Shake?" Movement down low caught her attention, and she suddenly realized that he was also missing his legs! There appeared to be a portion of a foot and toes sticking out which Gabe waved up and down as if trying to shake hands.

She felt like turning around and running away, but his voice pulled her back into the present.

"Gotcha! You know, before and after every chess game it's polite to shake hands. We can skip for now, but my foot works pretty well don't you think?"

Only then did April realize that there was a chessboard and pieces on a low table next to Gabe.

What, he plays chess? Before she could get over the thought, Gabe's voice interrupted again.

"Are you ready to start a game?"

Seeing April's blank look, Gabe paused and then turned to Cathy.

"Are you telling me that she doesn't know how to play?" he said then burst out laughing so hard he nearly fell out of his wheelchair.

April didn't know what to think, and Cathy just stood there with a twinkle in her eye.

April started feeling upset. "What's so funny? What are you laughing about?" she blurted out.

Between laughs, Gabe managed to say, "Cathy told me she was bringing a special needs friend to meet me today! From what I can see, you seem quite normal, if anything rather a beautiful friend. I guess that she meant you have a special need in that you don't know how to play chess!"

April forced a smile, and said "Can you really play chess? I thought..." her voice trailed off.

"Yes?" Gabe replied. "You mean you thought that since I'm in this classroom, I must be mentally not just physically different?"

Yeah, something like that, April thought, but all she could manage was a small nod.

Gabe's eyes suddenly turned more serious, and his voice was firm. "April, I think I know why Cathy invited you to come here," he said. "I wasn't always like this. I mean, mentally. Physically, yes, I was born this way. It really wasn't all that bad though because I have never known anything different. Perhaps it would have been harder if an accident had caused me to lose my arms and legs. Over time, I started to notice that people would look at me and turn away. They didn't know what to say. I also started to think that I couldn't do anything, that life itself wasn't even worth living. But then this game was introduced to me."

"Here, let me show you," he said and seemed to point with his chin to the chess set; then, using his toes, he pushed a few buttons that expertly moved his wheelchair in front of the set.

April sat down opposite him, but as she did, she bumped the table and pieces toppled over. "Oh, I'm sorry for being so clumsy!" she said.

"That's ok," Gabe replied with a smile. And to her shock, she saw him lean forward, and with his mouth and chin tip the pieces back upright, pushing them back into their squares on his side of the board. There was one that was a bit far away for him to reach, rather tall, with points around the top. April reached out and picked it up for him.

Gabe smiled and said, "Thank you."

"That's the queen," he said as she examined the chess piece. "It's the most powerful piece on the chess board. Would you like to learn how to play?"

April was about to say no then thought to herself, *that's pretty stupid. If he can play, maybe I can learn too.*

"Ok, let's start with the language of chess," Gabe said.

Before April could ask what he meant, Gabe continued. "Take a look at the chessboard. What do you notice?"

"Lots of squares," April said, "some light, some dark." "What else," Gabe said.

April looked again. "I don't see anything else unless you mean the chess pieces."

"No, not the pieces," he said. "Something else. Do you see the lines? Imagine the squares are lined up – do you see now? There are squares in lines forward and backward, or up and down, the board."

"Also, side to side," blurted out April, growing slightly more interested.

Gabe smiled brightly. "Exactly! Anything else?"

April looked closely when suddenly it popped into her mind, and she said more enthusiastically "Diagonals! The squares also form lines in diagonals."

"Nice work," said Gabe. "In chess language, the rows of squares forward and backward we call files; rows side to side we call ranks; and diagonals, well, they're just that, diagonals."

Gabe continued, "Something else really cool that helps a lot when talking about the game – see those small letters and numbers?" April looked closely and saw what Gabe was indicating. In front of her were the letters abcdefgh running left to right, and up each side of the board, she saw the numbers one through eight. "What are those for?" April asked, her interest continuing to grow.

"Those are how we can name every square on the board" Gabe replied. "The letters are how we name the files, and the numbers are how we name the ranks side to side. See that light-colored square in the corner to your right?"

April looked and pointed.

"That's right. What combination of letter and number could you use to name that square?" Gabe asked.

April looked carefully "h1?" She said it questioningly.

"You're right! Great job!" Gabe said with a big smile. "How about this dark square in the corner to my left?"

April looked again, "h8?"

"Well done!" Gabe exclaimed. "You've already learned the basic language for the chessboard and naming squares! High five?"

April happily swung her hand to give Gabe a high five and then paused.

"Gotcha again," Gabe laughed, and April chuckled just a bit as she realized that Gabe loved to use his lack of arms to make jokes.

April was eager to learn some more. "What's next? Can you tell me about the chess pieces? How do you play?"

"Happy to," Gabe replied. "Can you find the shortest pieces?" April moved all the pieces beside the board, separating them into light and dark, and carefully held up what she thought was the shortest piece.

Gabe replied, "We call that the pawn in chess. How many can you find?"

April quickly found all 8 of each color of pawn.

"The pawns start with the light pawns on the 2nd rank, and the dark pawns on the 7th rank" Gabe added. "Why don't you try setting them up?"

April started setting the pawns on their starting squares, slowly at first, then faster, till she had pawns filling the second and seventh ranks. She was starting to feel like maybe she could learn chess! It had always seemed so complicated and only something that brainiacs and nerds played. At least that's what she had always thought. Her world was a bit turned upside down, and she was rather enjoying it.

"Ok, that was fun! What's next?" April asked.

"Can you find the pieces that look a little like towers?" Gabe said. As April spotted one, Gabe continued "Those are called rooks – they start the game behind the pawns in the corners of the board."

As April started to place a dark rook on h1, Gabe interrupted. "Not that corner! You see, the light pieces all start on the 1st and 2nd ranks, the dark pieces on the 7th and 8th ranks."

April quickly moved the four rooks into position – white rooks on a1 and h1, dark rooks on a8 and h8.

"What's this called?" April was holding up a piece that looked like a horse's head.

"That's a knight," Gabe replied. "They sit next to the rooks at the start of the game."

April was eager to finish setting up the chess pieces. "Is this next?" She held up four pieces that matched in shape, with a rather pointy top.

"That's right," Gabe replied, "those are called bishops. Can you guess what squares they start on?"

April guessed correctly and placed them next to the knights.

April continued quickly, "Ok, just two more pieces. I already know the queen. What's this one with this 't' shape on top?"

"That's the king, and actually that's a cross on top," Gabe answered. "Remember the queen is the most powerful piece? Well, the king is the most important. Even though not as powerful as the queen, the game is over when the king is trapped and cannot escape. We call that checkmate!"

"Does it matter which squares they start on?" April asked as she placed the queen and king in the last two empty squares on the 1st rank.

"Yes, there is a little tip to remember," Gabe replied. "Just remember that the queen, being the most powerful, gets to start on a square of her same color. Light queen, light square – dark queen, dark square."

April switched the queens to their own color of squares and placed the kings in the remaining empty squares.

"Wow, that was a lot," she said. "I'm not sure I'm going to remember where these all go, let alone be able to play!"

"Oh, I'm sure you can," Gabe replied. "Here's another tip to remember how to set up the board: Pawns on ranks two and seven, then the back row makes a roof!"

April looked puzzled.

"Just lower your head to the level of the table," Gabe said. "What do you notice?"

April did so and then saw what Gabe meant. The rooks were the shortest pieces on the back row, and the pieces were progressively taller with the tallest pieces in the middle.

"That's cool!" she blurted out. Gabe just smiled happily.

"That's enough for now, April," Gabe said. "You've just learned how to set up the whole chessboard, and you've learned some of the chess language. Why don't you come back tomorrow and we can work on how the pieces move? I need to get some of my homework done."

April was startled again. Gabe doing homework? She hadn't thought...

"Did you think that perhaps special needs implies no ability?" Gabe said quietly, appearing to have read her thoughts! She turned red.

Gabe continued with a little smile, "Don't worry; it's ok, I'm used to it. People frequently assume that mental limitations go along with physical limitations. I can do my homework fine; it just takes me a while to complete."

As April walked out of the room, she looked back and was only slightly surprised to see Gabe now with a pencil in his mouth painstakingly writing answers in his homework notebook. She had a lot to think about and knew she would never think the same about the special needs end of the school.

April was very quiet as she walked towards the pickup zone where her mom would be waiting.

"What are you thinking?" Cathy's voice broke in on her thoughts, and she noticed that Cathy was there in the hallway, looking at her rather intently.

April blurted out, "How is that possible? I mean…" her voice trailed off as she tried to put into words the deep emotions she was feeling.

"Do you mean 'how is it possible that a young person with no arms and legs can actually play chess'?" Cathy replied.

"Well, yes…no…I don't know…I mean, he said that he wasn't always this way – yet he said he was born with no arms and legs – what happened?" April finally managed to say.

"Why don't you ask him tomorrow?" Cathy replied with a smile.

"I will," April said quietly.

As she lay in bed that night, April found herself reliving the afternoon over and over. Tomorrow couldn't come soon enough for her as she wondered what she would discover about Gabe.

CHAPTER 4

THE NEXT DAY April had a hard time staying focused on her teacher. The moment class was over, she hurried out of the classroom and headed down the hall towards Gabe's room.

"Where are you going in such a hurry?" said her classmate Teegan, who was known throughout the school for her teasing, often sarcastic comments. "Go too far that way you'll end up down in the special needs classroom – but maybe that's where you're headed after the soccer tryouts!" Teegan's words cut April deeper than she let on.

"Have to use the restroom and this one's less crowded," April called over her shoulder as she turned into the restroom usually avoided by students who felt awkward running into any of the students from the special needs classrooms. Not that she had to use the restroom, but it provided her a chance to privately regain her composure as the words from Teegan brought up some deep emotions, including the feeling that she was a failure, maybe even a disappointment to her parents.

It really had all started that night during the first week of school.

April had woken up to use the bathroom, and on her way back to bed, heard her parents' voices as she passed their room. She wasn't paying any attention but then hearing her name mentioned stopped, not realizing at first that she might be eavesdropping. "I'm really worried about what this means for April," her mother was saying. This was a surprise already, as Sara was nearly always positive and hopeful.

April had waited, listening.

"Well, I don't know what else to do, but it's just wrong! To be passed over AGAIN for the promotion after all the time I've put in – and that guy who has been here just one year getting the job I was in line for! Then on top of it, to be assigned to that ridiculous robotics line of products – it's like management just doesn't care at all about the hard work I've put in for all these years! And now look what it's doing to our family!" April's dad was obviously very frustrated. It wasn't the first time that April had heard her dad upset about management decisions at work, but this time there seemed to be something more intense in his voice.

"I just don't know – I'm not sure what we can do. Michael will do fine; look at his results in baseball tryouts. He'll for sure land a scholarship, but April, I just don't know. Without the advance that I should have gotten by now, I don't see a future at this company. Being stuck at this pay level, it just doesn't work!"

April heard her mom chime in quietly, "I just don't know how we can possibly afford a decent university for her, and, well, you know how difficult it can be without a solid degree," Sara's voice trailed off.

Davis continued, with emotion in his voice. "Her grades just aren't good enough to get a scholarship, and we can't afford a good university without help of some kind. I was really counting on the promotion to set aside funds for her!"

"Well, hopefully, it's just a matter of time – perhaps there is a better promotion coming our way," April's mom said.

April had suddenly realized she was standing there eavesdropping, and, not wanting to be discovered, quietly went to bed.

As she lay there, she had come up with an idea to help solve the problem. Her parents were worried about her, while her older brother Michael was on track to get a scholarship in baseball. Perhaps she could try out for the girls' soccer team and eventually earn a scholarship there. The idea wouldn't leave her, though she wasn't so sure she wanted to, as Teegan was on the team – Teegan, who lived just down the street and seemed to have a knack for making comments that made April feel awkward and like a failure.

Still, April had mustered her courage and gone to soccer tryouts, secretly hoping that she could somehow, miraculously, make it onto the team and eventually earn the scholarship. While she enjoyed kicking the soccer ball at home with her little brother, she wasn't sure she could make the team, but the dream of seeing the surprise and happiness on her parents' faces if she got the scholarship gave her enough courage to practice faithfully and go to the tryouts.

It was short-lived though, as, at the end of the very first tryout, the coach pulled her aside and quietly but kindly said to her, "I'm sorry April, I appreciate your trying out for soccer. However, I want you to know that we have a lot of experienced players to choose from, so I wanted to give you time to consider other options for sports sooner rather than later."

"Oh, that's ok," April said and walked away, just barely holding back her tears. She hadn't really thought she could make the team at first, but as she practiced, she had started to hope and dream just a little – and now the dreams were gone.

Since that day, April had been going through the motions of school and life, somewhat depressed, not really sure what direction to go, bearing this hidden burden of being a source of concern for her parents. She kept wishing there was a way to earn a scholarship for university, yet day after day not seeing a way, had all but given up hope.

April realized with a start that her eyes were wet with tears as she stood there in the restroom. Quickly dabbing her face with a little water, she wiped away any trace of the tears as best she could, and then headed out again. She hoped Teegan would be gone by now and wouldn't see her as she turned into the special needs classroom where Gabe was waiting.

"Did you forget how to use your legs?" Gabe grinned when April entered the room. "Took you so long to come, I thought maybe you needed some wheels to help out – or did you forget which classroom is for the smart kids?"

April didn't want to share what had happened on the way, so she dove right in with the question she had been thinking about. "Gabe, I've been wondering – what did you mean when you said you weren't always this way? What happened?"

Gabe's joking face turned rather somber as he appeared to be remembering something, then he slowly said, "Are you sure you want to know? It's a bit of a long story."

"Yes," she said. "Please do tell me!"

Gabe quietly began, "It was like this. You see, I was born in a small village in Eastern Africa. When I was born, my parents were shocked to see me without arms and legs, and VERY ashamed of me. They didn't know what to do – and many others like me have often been left to die, it's considered such a shameful thing. In fact, my father didn't want me at all and was so upset; he left my mom. My mom didn't know what to do, but she ended up hearing of this place where children with physical deformities or other challenges are taken care of. It's paid for by some very kind people. I was brought there and simply left on the doorstep. At least it was on the doorstep instead of in the bush to be left to die like so many others were.

"The home took me in, and though I am grateful for their kindness, still there were many challenges. You see, in my country, people usually shun these places. People in these homes are often seen as outcasts, worthless, and not able to do anything.

"One day, this man came in and talked with us. I could tell he loved us – he didn't look at us and just feel sorry for us – he looked at us with kindness in his eyes, spoke with us, and treated us as if we were normal! He's the one who brought in the chess game and introduced it to us.

"At first, we didn't think we could do it at all, but just like I showed you yesterday, he helped us learn the rules, one by one. Whenever one of us said 'I can't,' Coach (as we called him) would simply say 'If you say you can't, you can't – but if you say you can, you can!' I remember saying to him, 'But Coach, how can I play chess? Don't you see I don't have any arms? I can't move the pieces!' He simply looked at me and said, 'Gabe, your name is short for Gabriel who was an angel of God, and not just an angel – a mighty angel! Instead of seeing what you don't have, why don't you try to start seeing everything you do have? Let's see – you have a mouth and teeth, don't you Gabe? I can tell because you say so much!'

"Everyone laughed – then he said to me, 'Why don't you try it?' And I did! I learned to pick up chess pieces with my mouth. Another time he said, 'Gabe, you have part of a foot, don't you? God didn't give it to you so you could just use it for waving – what do you think you can do with it?'

"He kept encouraging me, and eventually I learned to use this partial foot to move the chess pieces around. I became rather handy at doing it. So much so that I like to call it my hand. Remember? Wanna shake?"

Gabe smiled again as he recalled April's shocked look when she first met him.

As Gabe shared his story, April felt as if she was right with him in the home. "What happened after that?"

"Coach taught us how to move the pieces," he said. "Here, let me show you what he showed us. Are you ready for the next chess lesson?"

April nodded eagerly, and Gabe wasted no time getting started.

Gabe indicated the board. "Remember how to set up the chessboard? Let's race – you set up all 16 of your pieces, I'll do mine."

April hurried to set up the pieces, remembering to form the roof on her chessboard, but couldn't help being distracted by how nimbly Gabe used his mouth, partial foot, and anything else he had including the pencil he held between his teeth.

April still finished first, but she admired Gabe's persistence as he completed setting up the pieces on his side. "Wow, that's amazing!" she blurted out.

Gabe simply smiled.

"So, what did Coach teach you next?" April was eager to learn more.

Gabe continued, "Well, once we all had learned how to set up the chessboards, some of the students said, 'Coach, that's too hard – we can't learn how all those pieces move! Only smart kids can do that'."

Coach replied, "Is that really true? Remember, if you think you can't, you can't. If you think you can," in unison the students finished, "you can!"

"That's right," Coach continued. "And guess what, if you think you're smart, you're – ?" He paused, and one student quietly finished the sentence 'You're smart.'

"Exactly," Coach said. "It's all in your head – and as far as I can tell, you all have heads, so I think we can do this!"

Everyone burst out laughing, and then one student said, "Coach, my head's the biggest. Does that make me the smartest?"

Coach laughed along with the students and added "Nice try, but it's not about how big your head is, it's about how you use what's inside it."

Gabe continued, "Week after week, Coach kept coming back, and each time he encouraged us to try something new. Not once did he ever show any doubt about our abilities, but simply expected us to all learn to play chess."

As Gabe described learning about how the pieces move and capture, April listened, captured by the story of how he, without arms or legs, had learned to play a game of many pieces.

Seeing April's interest, Gabe asked, "Would you like to learn how the king moves?"

"Yes!" April answered eagerly.

She quickly learned that the king gets to move one square in any direction yet is worth the whole game because trapping or checkmating the king ends a chess game.

April listened intently, and when Gabe finished explaining, she quickly removed all the pieces from the chessboard between her and Gabe, leaving just the kings. "Can I try?"

"Sure," said Gabe. "Just remember, before and after every game, shake hands with your opponent and say something nice such as 'have a good game' – it's what Coach taught us we should do to be a good sport." Then he added with a grin, "though in my case, it's usually 'shake my foot?'"

Gabe laughed a bit again.

April smiled and lightly shook 'hands' with Gabe's partial foot. Then she moved her king one square forward. While it took a while to play because of the time it took Gabe to push the piece with his partial foot or pencil in his mouth, at the same time she admired how he never gave up or seemed discouraged – he just kept trying until he got it – even when he bumped his piece over and had to use his mouth to pick it back up.

Gabe pushed his king forward with his foot, and they played a few moves. Once April was confident moving the king, Gabe moved on, teaching April one by one how to use the rook, the bishop, and then the pawns, letting April practice moving and capturing with each piece.

April learned that even though the king is worth the whole game, the other pieces each have a point value based on how they move. She learned that the queen being the most powerful piece is worth nine points, rooks are worth five points, knights and bishops each three points, and the weakest piece, the pawn, worth just one point because it could only move forward one square at a time.

As they practiced moving pawns, April commented, "I don't think I like pawns – they just can't seem to do much."

Gabe replied, "When Coach showed us how the pawns move, some students said the same thing. That's when Coach told us, 'Just because the piece looks small and weak, doesn't make the pawn unworthy – each piece has some unique ability, and pawns, even though they indeed appear weak, have a very special ability.'"

Gabe continued, "You see, while pawns indeed move only one square at a time, straight forward and indeed are stuck if something is in front of them blocking their movement, pawns actually get to capture other pieces if they are on a diagonal, as long as it's just one square away. All the other chess pieces capture the same way that they move, making this a unique ability for pawns."

Gabe looked off into space. "Coach said 'Just like each one of you. You may think at times that you are weak, but instead, learn to find your own unique ability that you have been given. Discover it – then use it. It will give you special opportunities if you do this.'" Gabe finished the retelling of his Coach's words of wisdom, smiling at his thoughts.

Breaking out of his reverie, Gabe continued. "You know, April, pawns are rather funny pieces. Even though they are the weakest piece because they only get to move forward, not backward or sideways, they have a couple of really cool things about them."

"Like you!" blurted out April, then she turned red again. "I mean…I mean…"

"That's ok," Gabe smiled, "you're right. I am different. With my own unique ability. How many people do you know who can shake hands with a foot?"

He laughed at his own joke, and April was relieved that he wasn't offended by her comment.

"That was fun!" April exclaimed when they had completed a game of practice with just pawns on the board.

"Ok, what's next?" April was excited about learning how the remaining pieces moved, as there were still left the queen and knight.

"That's all for today, April," Gabe replied, "I'm sorry, but I do have some homework, and I'm guessing your ride is here to take you home."

April couldn't believe how fast the time had flown by. "I was having so much fun learning about chess; I just realized you still haven't told me what happened to change you, Gabe."

"Why don't you come next week?" Gabe said. "We have an early release day on Wednesday, and you can hear all about it then!" April went home wishing it was Wednesday already. As she thought about Gabe's story, she found herself thinking of more questions. How did Gabe go from living in eastern Africa to now being in school in America? What happened? She couldn't wait to ask.

CHAPTER 5

WEDNESDAY CAME EVENTUALLY, and when class was over, April nearly ran to the special needs room in her eagerness to see Gabe.

"Trying out for track?" Teegan asked, but her remark didn't stop April.

"Why yes, want to join me?" April asked, leaving a rather bewildered Teegan to wonder what was happening to April.

April paused only momentarily to put a few items in her locker, then continued down the hall.

As she entered the special needs classroom, April immediately spotted Gabe. "So what happened? How did you come from that home in Africa to this school here?" April asked him, talking before she even sat down.

Gabe smiled. "Well, you'll find out soon – but to find out, we need to first learn the rest of the pieces in chess!"

April was puzzled. "But why, I don't see."

"That's ok," Gabe replied. "Just follow along, and I think you'll understand."

After a short review to make sure April remembered what she had learned the time before, Gabe continued with the lesson.

"Now, are you ready to learn about the queen? The queen is the most powerful piece in chess. She moves in any direction, just like the king; however, the queen can move one square or as many squares as she wants to!"

April's eyes were riveted on the queen's crown as her thoughts wandered for a moment, imagining herself wearing a college graduation cap as proudly as the chess queen appeared to wear the crown.

"Ready to practice moving and capturing with the queen?" Gabe said, interrupting April's daydreaming. "Yes," she said and focused again on the chessboard in front of her.

After several moves with the queen, Gabe smiled and said, "You're doing very well, April! You have learned very quickly how to move your most powerful piece!"

April sighed with satisfaction and Gabe was ready to move on. "Okay, you ready for the last piece?" he asked her. April happily nodded.

Gabe smiled. "This last piece, the knight, is actually my favorite piece." April was a bit surprised and couldn't help but ask "Why is it your favorite? Isn't the queen worth the most?"

Gabe answered quickly, "Yes, you're right about the queen being worth the most – but the knight has some very special unique abilities. You see, the knight is the only chess piece that has the power to jump over other pieces! It can be a bit confusing at first, but maybe that's part of why I like it the best." After a pause, Gabe added a little more quietly, "Maybe also because I see myself in it."

"What do you mean?" April asked.

"Well," Gabe replied, "when Coach came and taught us how the knight moves, he said, 'you could say that the knight has obstacles in front of it, many obstacles – and yet, what happens? It can simply jump right over those obstacles when they seem too difficult to get through them! How often in your life do you see the obstacles in front of you and think 'I can't get through this!' Well, just learn how to jump over!'"

That would be wonderful, April mused. "So how exactly does the knight move?"

"One, two, and sideways one square," Gabe said, "Just like an L shape. And just remember that it jumps to the square, moving over any pieces in between!"

"That's exciting!" April exclaimed. "I can see now why you like the knight. I think I'm going to like it too."

As they played a practice game moving knights, jumping and capturing, April suddenly said, "Oh, I almost forgot again! You said I would learn about how you came to the U.S. as we learned how the pieces move – but I don't know yet. What happened?"

Gabe smiled and then thought for a moment before saying, "There is something else you need to learn, and then you will understand."

"Please tell me!" April couldn't wait to find out. Gabe launched into his story.

"After Coach showed us how the pieces move, I sat there one day feeling quite sad. I didn't see how this all could help me, and I wasn't really sure I could actually play chess. Yes, maybe I could move some pieces, but it seemed to me that I wasn't good enough. Coach seemed to know what I was thinking – he was like that, always seemed to understand what each student was feeling – and came up and said to me, 'Gabe, let me guess. Are you feeling like you're just a pawn in life?' I was startled at how well he understood. 'Well, yes, that's kind of how I feel,' I answered. 'I so often feel stuck; I can't move, I'm slow without legs and arms…and even if I can get to the other side of the board, then I'm hopelessly stuck forever until someone comes and captures me. It feels hopeless! I can't do this.'

Coach listened and was quiet for a bit. 'Gabe,' he said, 'there are two more rules of chess I haven't shared yet, but I think it's time for you to learn them. Remember I said that each piece has a unique ability that no other piece has?'

'Yes, Coach,' I said.

'Well,' he said, 'there is hidden within you a unique ability that is waiting to be discovered. So, in life, you feel like you're 'just' a pawn? Look, in chess, there is another rule about pawns. What direction can pawns move?'

I answered him. 'Only forward. Except when capturing; then they can move diagonally.'

'Good,' he said. 'And how many squares do they move?' 'Just one,' I muttered.

'That's right,' he said, 'but guess what happens when a pawn reaches the opposite side of the board?'

'Well, it's just stuck, isn't it?' I replied.

'Actually no,' Coach continued. 'When a pawn reaches the last row, what happens in chess is that the pawn is replaced by one of the other pieces – knight, bishop, rook, or even another queen! You see, the pawn 'PROMOTES' and becomes another piece, a powerful piece, of your choice.'

Coach lowered his voice as he looked directly into my eyes. Then he told me something that has made all the difference to me in my life and in the game. He said, 'In chess, the Little One can become the BIG one! It is your choice! What do you want to become? You can do it – and hidden within you is the unique ability that God has gifted you with. There is something within you that must be discovered and understood so that it may be fully utilized, but it is something that can be discovered as long as you have the attitude that you can.'

'Why do I say it this way?' Coach continued. 'Because if you think you can't – you're right, you can't. As a pawn, you can just be captured before you get across the board. But if you think you can, you can. So why not do your best, and trust that God who gave you your unique ability will help you become the ONE that you dream of becoming?'"

"I was struck by what he said. For the first time in my life, I felt that indeed this was true! There was something great inside me, April! For my whole life, I had seen what I didn't have, and my attitude of 'can't' had held me back. Now, I was just beginning to realize that if I had a Can-Do Attitude, nearly anything would be possible!"

Gabe was silent for a bit, and April also felt the depth of what Gabe had shared. She wondered about her own unique ability, feeling the truth in his words, and starting to think about what could be in her own life. After a bit, her thoughts returned to Gabe.

"But how did you come to the United States?" April wondered aloud.

"Well," Gabe continued, "with my new-found courage, I had a thought. Coach had talked about a chess tournament where students competed, and I thought 'what if I work at practicing and improving my chess – maybe I can become good enough to play in the tournament someday!' With this dream, I started playing every day and trying to get better. I would ask Coach questions every time he was there, and when he wasn't there, I would play anyone willing to play. For a while, I usually lost, but over time I started winning games.

"One day, Coach came to me during club and said, 'Gabe, would you like to play in the chess tournament?' In some ways, I couldn't believe my ears. Yet in other ways, I knew it was coming – because I had started to see myself as that little pawn that was slowly advancing across the board, getting closer and closer to becoming a 'big one'!

"That first tournament led to another tournament, and then another. Then one day Coach came to me again with a question, 'Gabe, are you ready for your biggest challenge and perhaps your biggest opportunity yet?'

"'I don't know if I'm ready, Coach, but I will do my best,' I said. 'What is it?'

"I learned from Coach that there was to be an international

tournament for physically disabled students and that a gentleman in the United States offered a scholarship to the winner of that event – a scholarship that would enable the recipient to attend a university in the U.S. This scholarship covered travel, tuition, and living expenses related to attending high school through the first four years of university."

Gabe paused. April could tell he was struggling to keep back his emotions.

"So you see," he said, "that in short, is the reason I am here – because of Coach who believed in each of our unique abilities, who instilled in us the CAN DO attitude; because of another person who cared enough to use his wealth helping others; and especially because of the God who gave each one of us this hidden unique ability."

"Thank you very much for sharing," April said quietly as she dabbed at her wet eyes. "That was amazing. Wow, Gabe, do you know, I don't think I will ever see someone again as disabled – maybe just as 'differently-abled.'"

"I'm glad to hear it," Gabe said.

April mulled over what Gabe had told her and went looking for Cathy. She found her leaving the gym and fell in step with her.

"Do you have a minute for me?" April asked. "Yes, happy to," Cathy said. "What is it?"

April asked, "Did you want me to visit Gabe to learn that what matters most is not what I have outside, but what I have inside – the CAN DO attitude?"

"Yes indeed," Cathy said smiling, as they walked towards the school's main exit.

April suddenly stopped short. "What's the matter?" Cathy asked.

"What do you think? I have learned to play chess. If I practiced enough, do you suppose I could also maybe earn a scholarship?"

Cathy smiled. "I think you know the answer."

April softly repeated, "If you think you can, YOU CAN. If I think I can, I can!!"

She felt as if she was floating on air, and hope was high as she rode home. That night she dreamt about winning a chess tournament, with a full scholarship as part of the prize – and then going on to university afterward perhaps! She woke once and thought, *I'm not going to tell anyone, but keep it a secret with Cathy.* She was sure she could do it. After all, if Gabe could, why not her?

With that, she turned over and went to sleep again – little dreaming of the challenges that were about to appear.

CHAPTER 6

APRIL AWOKE THE next morning feeling more hopeful than she recalled feeling in a long time. She lay still, wondering why – then recalled the feelings of the day before and her exciting thoughts of going to university on a chess scholarship. She jumped out of bed, eager to get started – though not really sure how to begin! She remembered what Gabe had said about Coach bringing books and the students practicing together. *I know. I'll just head to the library and see what I can find there!* With that thought, April jumped out of bed and dressed quickly.

Visions of winning a chess tournament were floating through her mind as she entered the kitchen with her coat already on, eager to get to the library and find some chess books.

"Good morning, April!" Sara said without turning from the stove where she was busy making breakfast. "You're up early! Did you sleep ok?"

"Yes. I was just ready to get up," April said as she sat down at the table; Max was already sitting there eating his toast in his usual style – with more crumbs ending up on the floor than on his plate, it seemed.

As Sara placed a steaming dish of scrambled eggs on the table, she noticed April's coat with surprise. "Are you feeling sick?" She reached over to check April's forehead for a potential fever.

"I was just thinking I would go to the library for a bit," April replied, not about to share her plan to find some chess books and start reading them. She was unsure how her family would react to the idea.

"I see," her mom replied. "I'm really sorry April, but I need you to stay home and watch Max for me – I need to go out this morning to pick up some new student success workbooks since the school supply store has a special sale on. Perhaps you can go after I return?"

April was quite disappointed but tried not to show it. "How long will you be gone?"

"I'll do my best to be back around lunchtime. However, if I'm late, there are leftovers in the fridge you can warm up for lunch," Sara said. She gathered her keys and headed towards the door.

April's heart sank a bit more. There was a good chance that with how things usually worked out, her mom would be home later than she expected, leaving very little time to carry out her plan for the day of finding chess books at the library, let alone reading them while there. She wasn't about to check the books out, bring them home, and then have to explain why she was suddenly interested in chess.

"Can't Michael take care of Max today?" April asked, though not really expecting her mother to agree. Michael was a senior, and between maintaining his excellent grades, attending baseball practice, and managing his newly added role as president of the robotics club, he seemed to be busy all the time; and it seemed to April that taking care of Max was always her responsibility.

"I've got homework I need to focus on completing this morning, then I've got practice from 11 till 2, and after that I need to open up the new robot kit before I bring it to the Robotics Club at school Monday," Michael said as he entered the room, quickly filling a plate with food, and not even stopping to sit down as he headed back to his room.

"Will Dad be home today?" April said, trying one last attempt at finding a way to get herself to the library.

"Dad left early this morning," Sara said. "He had to go back in to take care of some work issues that didn't get cleared up this week."

It seemed to April that her dad was nearly always gone working – he was rarely home for dinner more than twice during the week, and at least every other weekend he was gone working on one project or another. To April it seemed that he didn't have time to come to any of her school events, although he somehow managed to make it to almost all of Michael's baseball games and even many of his practices. Sometimes April wondered if her Dad would have come to her events if she had made it onto the soccer team.

Maybe Dad will come if I win the chess scholarship! April thought… then corrected herself. *WHEN I win the chess scholarship! If I think I can…I can!*

With this thought, April brightened up and decided she would just do the best she could and hope that her mom got back soon enough for her to at least get started on her plan.

After Sara left, April cleaned up the kitchen, washing the dishes as well as sweeping up the crumbs, then headed outside, where Max was already playing with his soccer ball.

Kicking the ball back and forth lasted for about half an hour, and then Max was ready for a change.

"Do you want to learn how to play chess?" April asked. "I've done that already," Max said.

"You know how to play chess?" April was surprised. "Of course! I won my class challenge!" Max replied. April was even more surprised. "You what?"

"I got first a few weeks ago," Max replied matter-of-factly.

Apparently, to him, it was nothing out of the ordinary to not only be playing chess but also to win!

April started to feel as if both her brothers, older and younger, were the achievers and that she was left out. But then her little brother said something that made her reconsider.

"Teacher started this thing she calls 'STEAM Time,' and once a week we do a special activity in the hour. We've been playing chess for a while now, and one time I took first place! I got all the pieces set up right the fastest!"

April felt a bit relieved as she realized that her brother had only finished first in setting up the chess board.

"Well, do you want to play chess then?" April asked. "Girls can't play chess," Max said.

"Why do you say that?" April asked.

"I don't know – they just can't," Max said.

"Well, how about we try anyway?" April was secretly glad now that her mom was gone and she was able to play Max without anyone else in the family seeing.

Not having anyone else to play with, Max agreed.

They went into the house and Max ran to his room, returning quickly with a small vinyl chessboard about 14 inches square along with a small bag of chess pieces.

April hadn't seen the set before. "Where did you get that?" "Everyone in my class got one as soon as we learned how all the pieces move!" Max replied. April realized that Max was actually telling the truth, not just letting his imagination tell a story (as he sometimes did).

"Ok, you ready to race?" Max asked. "Remember, I'm the champion!"

"Sure thing," April said. "Ready, Set, Go!"

They raced to set up the pieces, and to April's surprise, Max was quite fast and accurate! It was all April could do to keep up with him, and Max finished first while April was still trying to remember which squares the king and queen sit on to begin the game.

"I win! I win!" Max jumped up and down.

Max seemed to forget "girls can't play chess" as he was eager to start the chess game, and they played together for a while, with Max happily counting the points every time he captured one of April's pieces and announcing quite loudly how many 'points' he had captured so far in the game. April didn't capture nearly as many, but she was pleased that she was remembering to look for captures herself and even managed to take Max's queen at one point. Once that happened, Max looked disappointed and appeared to lose interest quickly. "Let's do something else!" he said after just a couple more moves.

April wanted to continue the game, but she knew from experience that crossing Max would likely result in a lengthy losing battle, so she decided to humor him.

"Sure, what would you like to do?" April said, and then with a start, she realized it was nearly lunchtime.

"How about you go find something else while I get lunch going?"

Max darted off without even replying – something April was quite used to as he had a habit of jumping from one thing to another rather rapidly.

As she fixed lunch, April started daydreaming once again about winning at chess. She hoped her mom would come back soon.

"Ow!" Max's yell and a rather loud 'crunching sound' brought April back to the present. She ran to find out what trouble Max had gotten himself into this time.

"What happened?" April called as she followed the sounds to Max's room. She found him sitting on the floor, next to a torn box, surrounded by many pieces and random parts that seemed to belong to something, although she wasn't sure what.

"Oh no! Not that!" April burst out as her eye caught part of the label from the box: "Robotics Kit - HANDLE WITH CARE - DANGER - SMALL PARTS - KEEP AWAY FROM YOUNG CHILDREN."

"Where did you find this?" she asked, trying not to step on any parts while coming closer to inspect Max's injury.

Max rubbed his foot, apparently having stepped on one of the parts. "It was in Dad's office – you know he's always bringing home new toys. I thought it was another toy we could look at."

It was true that her Dad often brought home toys that were part of his product line at work, and he often asked his children to play with them and give feedback on what they liked or didn't like about them – but April wasn't so sure about this new robotics line, and she had a feeling that her Dad would not be too happy about this package being torn open.

"Here, let's clean this up then go eat lunch," April said.

"Ow, it still hurts!" Max replied, a tear threatening to roll down his cheek.

April pushed a few parts out of the way, sat on the floor, and rubbed Max's foot. "There, is that better?"

Max nodded.

"Let's put the parts into this box," April said and started to pick up the tiny parts.

Max joined in, helping her carefully place all the parts into the half of the box that was still intact.

April took the box to her room, not quite sure what else to do with it until she would have a chance to tell her Dad about it. She hoped he wouldn't be too upset, but she had a feeling this might be an expensive item.

April's mom surprised her by returning while they were still finishing lunch. "Thank you for taking care of Max this morning," her mom said. "I'm home the rest of the day, so feel free to go to the library if you still wish to."

Sara loved books herself and believed that reading was a key to progress, so she was happy that April showed interest in reading, though if she had known what kind of books April had in mind, she probably would have been more than a little surprised.

When April arrived at the library, it took her a while to find the chess books, as she really didn't feel like asking someone. She wondered, *what if girls really can't play chess?* The thought troubled her for a bit, but she wasn't about to give up that easily yet, and besides, she reminded herself, Max is only nine, so he probably just picked up that idea somehow like he sometimes got other strange ideas.

The number of chess books on the shelf surprised her just a little. She had no idea really what to expect but to see a full row made her feel both surprised and a little intimidated. Are there really this many books on playing chess? I wonder if it's too hard for me, she thought. Then she pushed away the thought and decided to jump right in with the first book she picked up.

It was titled "How to Beat Your Dad at Chess," and she thought, *'that's cool' – I'm not sure if Dad plays, but he probably knows how, and if I could beat him someday, maybe he would be interested to see me compete in a chess tournament!*

The book just didn't make much sense to her though, so after a bit, she put it back and picked up the next one. "Learn from the Masters" was the title. *Maybe this will help – 'master' sounds like a good player – if I learn this, perhaps I can win easily!* April thought. This time the book was even more confusing, with lists of chess moves which didn't make any sense to her – pages and pages of diagrams of positions. She had no idea what was happening! She put the book back, feeling a bit discouraged.

After looking at another half-dozen chess books with similar results, April felt like giving up her quest. Just then she spotted another book titled "Bobby Fischer Teaches Chess." She liked the sound of that book, and when she opened it, she saw it was filled with diagrams of chess positions with simple questions for each position. Finally, she had found a book on chess that she could understand at least a little bit! She decided to check it out and then ask Gabe as soon as possible if he had some recommendations. She knew there was the risk of her family seeing that she had checked out the book but figured that she could hide it with her school books if need be.

The next Monday after school April took the chess book with her to Gabe's classroom but was quite disappointed to find the room empty. She wondered if Gabe would return soon and decided to wait for a little. Seeing the ever-present chess set on the table, April sat down and opened the book. She carefully set up on the chessboard one of the positions in the book, and then worked hard to figure out the answer. Once she had what she thought was the correct answer, she turned the page to check her answer and sure enough she had solved it correctly! Feeling good about finding the right answer, April set up and solved the questions for several more diagrams in the book... but soon found herself with positions that she had no idea how to solve.

"Hi! I wasn't expecting to see you here!" Cathy's voice surprised April. "What are you doing? Working on winning the chess scholarship?" Cathy's tone showed no doubt about this possibility and made it sound as if it was something she fully expected April to achieve.

"Well, yes, I thought that if I found some chess books, it would help me learn and be ready to compete – but it's so confusing! I went to the library, and there were so many chess books, but I couldn't figure out what they meant. I found this one book and decided to ask Gabe if he had some recommendations. I don't know where he is though. I started working on a few puzzles in this book, but it's rather confusing! And there are so many books! I don't know what to do!" April's voice, as much as her words, showed how overwhelmed she was feeling.

Cathy smiled as she sat down. "I was coming to check in with Gabe also on a couple of things, but since he's not here right now, would you like to hear a bit more about the chess scholarships?"

April nodded, wanting to know more, though still feeling

discouraged by the difficulty of the chess books at the library and even her slow progress in the one book she had tried learning from.

"You're feeling a little discouraged, aren't you?" Cathy seemed to have a knack for realizing what she was feeling.

April nodded slowly.

"I'll fill you in about the scholarships in a little bit, but I think there's something else quite important first. Do you remember the lesson you learned from Gabe?" Cathy asked.

April slowly nodded and replied, "If you think you can't, you can't – if you think you can, you can."

"Exactly," Cathy said. "However, this attitude, while crucial to have, by itself is not sufficient. April, you have a wonderful dream, and I believe you can indeed achieve it. However, when you have a dream as big as yours, there are more skills you need to develop to achieve it. I like to call these the 'fundamental life skills' because just like in soccer where you need to learn the fundamentals of ball control, passing, and kicking before you can succeed in a game, in life, also, there are certain fundamental skills that are essential to achieving your dreams.

"The Can-Do Attitude is one of those life skills. You've discovered this already through meeting Gabe and learning how to play chess. What I've got here is a tool that may help with your journey. I call this the 'Chart of Champions.' Would you like to see it?"

April nodded eagerly and leaned forward to see it, but when Cathy handed her the paper, April was disappointed and rather puzzled – all she saw was a page titled "Chart of Champions" and a row of empty boxes rather like a spreadsheet.

Cathy smiled and said, "Let me explain. As you discover the fundamental life skills, you can fill in the blanks. Next to each of them, there is room for you to add notes on insights as you make progress. Here at the top, you can fill in the life skill you already learned."

April quickly wrote in the top box Can-Do Attitude. "What's the next one?" She asked Cathy eagerly. "Goal Setting" Cathy replied.

April looked puzzled. "Is that really a life skill? It seems like it's really easy to set a goal."

"You're right that it seems really easy to set a goal," Cathy replied. "But that's just it – many people set goals, but because they do not set them effectively, they often fail to achieve them. In fact, many goals are really nothing more than dreams.

You probably felt rather overwhelmed looking at all those books and perhaps felt a little bit like your dream of winning a chess scholarship was just that, a dream only?" Cathy asked.

"Yes," April said, "that's exactly how I felt."

Cathy continued, "So you see, April, Goal Setting as a life skill is really about learning to take a dream and turn it into a SMART goal."

"What do you mean, a smart goal?" April interrupted. "SMART is simply an acronym or word in which each letter stands for something – it's a way to remember a concept easily. This SMART goal setting is something that is used in many areas. Would you like to learn what it stands for in relation to your goal of winning a chess scholarship?" Cathy added.

"Yes! Please help me understand!" April was eager to learn how to make her dream a reality.

Cathy explained, "The "S" in Smart stands for "Specific." It's very important that you know exactly what your goal is!"

"What do you mean?" April said. "Isn't winning a chess scholarship to college specific enough?"

"Which college? Which tournament has the scholarship? What section of the tournament? What are the requirements to win the scholarship?" Cathy replied. "You see what I mean about needing to be more specific?"

April nodded slowly. "You're saying that basically without

knowing exactly what the goal is, how do I know what to do to achieve it?"

"That's right," Cathy said and then added, "There are a growing number of opportunities available including universities offering scholarships for chess. It appears that at the national championships they may give out several of these scholarships! However, to win the national championships requires achieving a very high level of chess expertise. Since you're just getting started, there are some other possibilities. For example, there is a scholarship for 'top girl' in the state scholastic championships, plus there are a growing number of scholarships being made available through what is called STEM education."

"My younger brother mentioned STEAM Time in his class – does that have anything to do with it?" April interrupted.

"Yes," Cathy said, "STEM is another acronym, that stands for Science, Technology, Engineering, and Math. STEAM adds an 'A' as it is considered by many that Art is also an essential component. The goal behind these initiatives is to help children develop skills to help succeed in the world we live in, where an understanding of computers and technology is rapidly becoming essential."

"Back to the scholarships though! While the majority of scholarships traditionally still go to athletes, this year there are a number of STEM-related scholarships, plus a couple of substantial chess scholarships that can be earned."

"Do you think there is one that I would have a chance of winning this year?" April was eager to learn more about the chess scholarships.

"Well, yes, I do believe you do indeed have a chance, April," Cathy replied. "One of the scholarships that it seems to me would be a SMART goal to aim for is the one that is being offered for the top finisher among girls at this year's state championships. However, let me explain the rest of the SMART acronym in order for you to understand why I think so even though you've just begun learning chess."

"After the S for Specific, M stands for Measurable," Cathy continued. "Here's how you could measure this. In chess, if you compete in tournaments, you earn a chess rating that goes up or down as you win or lose – higher is better. If you were to look at the rating of the person that won a tournament last year, you would have a good idea of how high your rating needs to be in order to have a good chance of winning the tournament. As you learn and practice along the way, you can measure your progress towards that rating target."

Cathy smiled as she added, "Another very clear way to measure your success on this goal is simply winning the tournament!"

"That sounds exciting!" April replied. "What's next?"
"Achievable," Cathy replied. "You see, you have to believe that you can actually achieve it, or it's not likely to happen. And to ensure it is achievable, you need a basis to determine how achievable it is."

"You mean just like the 'Can-Do Attitude'?" April asked. "Yes, very similar to that."

Cathy went quickly through the rest of the SMART Acronym, talking about the importance of each of the elements and how they worked together: Specific, Measurable, Achievable, Realistic, and Timely.

When she finished, April sat still, thinking about what she had just heard.

Cathy waited, giving April time to digest it.

April finally spoke, "I think I now understand what you mean by saying that Goal Setting is much more than simply having a dream of achievement. I can see that I have a lot to think about to be very clear about my goal if I'm going to stand a good chance of winning the scholarship."

The initial excitement April had felt as she dreamed of winning a college scholarship and thought of the surprise her parents would experience was slowly waning – but in its place, she felt a growing resolve that even though it was going to take a lot of work, she would give it her all and win one of the scholarships.

Cathy again seemed to sense what April was feeling, and as April filled in the second box on her Chart of Champions with "Goal Setting," she said to her, "You're making really good progress, April! Would you like a recommendation for how you can improve your chess skill rapidly?"

"I would love that!" April said eagerly.

"Come over here," Cathy said and led April to the library computers. After logging in, Cathy showed April a website that had the phrase "Life Skills Through Chess" displayed prominently on it. "This is a tool that you can use anywhere you can go online, at home or at school during free time."

Cathy showed April where to log in and how to go step-by-step through the online video lessons as well as the activities and puzzles attached to every lesson.

"April," Cathy said, "as long as you consistently practice this content in the order recommended and don't skip any of the activities or puzzles, you will make rapid progress."

"Thank you, Cathy! This looks very good – and fun too!" April said. "If I have questions, do you think Gabe could help me also?"

"That's a great idea," Cathy said, "why don't you ask him next week since it appears that he's probably gone home already today."

As they left the classroom together, April asked, "What's the next life skill on the Chart of Champions?"

Cathy smiled again. "Let's leave that for you to discover – see if you can figure out another one."

When April arrived back home, she slipped quietly into her bedroom and posted the Chart of Champions inside her closet where she figured no one would see it – she knew that she still wasn't ready to share with her family the journey that she was on. Then, as she sat there quietly by herself, she thought about everything she had learned that day. She was excited about the online web program to help her learn more. She also had the sense that this journey she was on was going to take much more than she had originally thought – but she was determined to succeed.

I wonder what the next life skill is and when I'll discover it, she thought as she drifted off to sleep that night.

She didn't have long to wait to find out.

CHAPTER 7

THE NEXT WEEK seemed to fly by. Eager to get to her chess practice online, April applied herself more than ever before during the school day, doing her best to finish her homework during class time. Her teachers were pleased if mystified by the change, not sure what had come over April and hoping it would last.

Every moment she could find, April went to the computer lab and worked through the online course, motivated even more by seeing her progress tracker move forward after every puzzle she solved. Sometimes there would be a concept that stumped her, but she found that Gabe was a great resource and happy to help explain whenever she asked.

Still, anytime someone came near, April switched from the chess program to her homework folder – she couldn't let others in on her aspirations yet. While she probably didn't put it into words, there was still an underlying fear that perhaps her dream would be shattered if others knew about it, or maybe it was a fear of what others might think (perhaps it was true what Max had said, that "Girls can't play chess"). Either way, April kept her progress in chess to herself, with the exception of Gabe and, of course, Cathy. Maybe to some, it would have seemed unusual for April to be confiding in Cathy; then again, maybe it wouldn't have been seen as unusual since it was Cathy!

Cathy seemed to break most molds. She had a way of asking questions that were not comfortable. She questioned things which had been done for decades – and especially challenged anyone who answered her questions with "Well, that's how it's been done." Yet at the same time her warm smile, bright eyes, and unshakeable belief that everyone wants to help make things better had a way of causing others to believe also. Through that belief, she often accomplished far more than they ever thought possible. She appeared to have unlimited energy – and the only times she was ever heard to lose patience was when she came face-to-face with someone who appeared to block progress and care about self-interest instead of what was best for the children.

When Cathy had come to April's school district a few years before, the hiring team were quite relieved to finally have someone willing to fill the enrichment programs coordinator role; a role too readily looked down on as glorified daycare rather than education. They might have been less relieved if they had realized what they were getting themselves into by hiring Cathy.

In just a few years, Cathy had revamped many enrichment programs – from art, music, and debate to more recently her focus on STEM programs. It wasn't obvious how she had done so. Perhaps it was the excellence that she seemed to expect from everyone, whether a first-time student or the tenured teacher, a parent volunteer or a special needs student. No, she did not expect perfection – but she did expect every person to do their very best, measure the progress made, learn from mistakes, and strive for excellence. "Do, or do not – there is no try," she would often say impersonating the famous Yoda – leading some to say with a smile that perhaps she came right out of Star Wars with her 'beyond normal' ideas.

It was not uncommon for other staff to say, "I wonder what she'll be up to next." Yet in spite of some raised eyebrows regarding the methods, no one could deny that Cathy's efforts, by whatever methods or magic, were producing results - attendance improving, fewer absences, parent/teacher conferences no longer something to be dreaded, and the 'holy grail' of student scores displaying upward progress.

True, it would be difficult to attribute the results directly to Cathy's efforts alone, but it's possible that the results had something to do with Cathy's undying belief that every person has a seed of greatness inside of them. Just as April had learned through her experience with Gabe, Cathy believed that every person has a unique ability that is just waiting to be developed, and in many cases, first discovered and then developed. Cathy felt that no matter what a person has been through in the past, their future is boundless, with the only obstacle being a self-imposed limiting belief.

Her wish for more girls to learn chess and be involved in STEM programs gave additional incentive for her to see April succeed. Wanting to continue encouraging April, Cathy made time to check in with her on Friday and found her in the computer lab.

"April how is your chess progressing?" Cathy asked as she looked at the chess position on the screen.

April looked up from the computer screen where she was solving a checkmate challenge puzzle and smiled. "I'm really enjoying this – it's going great – I think I can really do this!"

Cathy smiled. "Well, would you like to come to next week's chess club meeting preparing students for the upcoming tournament? You'll be able to learn the tournament rules plus play in the practice rounds. What do you think? Would you like to go?"

"I would love to!" April said. She was rather surprised at herself as she was not usually that enthusiastic about trying new things – but the success she felt as she learned chess gave her the courage to say yes.

"Great!" Cathy said and smiled, pleased indeed to see April's willingness to take on the challenge. "The chess club will be meeting next week Wednesday after school in the multi-purpose room. I'll leave you to stay focused on practicing."

Over the next several days, April intensified her efforts to improve her chess skills, her confidence growing along with her increasing chess knowledge. Just to be safe, she checked in with Gabe the day before the club's practice session to ask him about any tips he could give her.

"Take your time every move and remember to have fun," was Gabe's simple advice. "See you tomorrow!"

April was pleasantly surprised, "You're going to come too?" "Of course, why wouldn't I?" Gabe replied.

That was stupid of me, April thought to herself, *of course, he would be coming – he won a chess tournament which led to his coming to this school – naturally, he would be there. She realized that somehow it was still difficult for her to think of a special needs student participating in an event that so-called normal students would be playing in.*

After school Wednesday, April headed over to the multi-purpose room, where she found a couple dozen students of varying ages already busily setting up chessboards. The math teacher who regularly volunteered to lead the chess club was also there, setting up a large roll-up board that was hung on a hook on the wall.

April was surprised to see a number of elementary and middle school-aged students present as well as the high school chess club members, and even more surprised when Max came running up to her saying in a rather loud voice, "April! What are you doing here? Girls can't play chess!"

April replied, "What are YOU doing here, Max? Aren't you supposed to be riding the bus home? How did you get here?"

Max answered, "Oh, my class was invited to join the chess prep session and Mom said it was ok to come over – she said she'll come and pick me up here today."

April paused, suddenly a bit dismayed – there were just a couple of girls in the room besides her! Maybe girls just aren't good at chess – the thought forced its way into her mind as the confidence she had felt all week suddenly drained away.

A bit timidly she approached the teacher. "Excuse me," she said.

"Yes?" He replied without looking up. "What can I help you with?"

"Do girls play chess?" she finally blurted out.

He turned around as he placed the last piece on its starting position. "Well, you're here, aren't you?" He said and smiled. "Don't worry; you'll do just fine. It's not what's outside that counts, it's only what's inside that matters." He tapped his head with one finger as he spoke. "Here, would you like to help me? You can take this stack of papers and hand them out to each of the students here."

April was happy to help and felt a little better, though still unsure. As she handed out the papers to the rest of the students, she read the title: "Tournament Prep, Rules & Tips for Success."

Just as the teacher was calling the class to attention, in came Gabe in his wheelchair, followed by, of all people, Teegan.

Oh no, thought April, *I hope she doesn't see me.* April really didn't want Teegan to know she was there to play chess – she could just imagine the kind of comments Teegan could come up with.

"Hi, April!" Gabe called out and flashed a smile at her. Teegan also looked up and the surprise on her face at seeing April showed. "You're here?" Teegan asked, "What do you think you're doing – think you're smart or something? Or just checking out the cute guy over there?" And Teegan nodded her head in the direction of the group of high school boys.

April didn't know what to say, so she just said, "Well, what are you doing here?"

"I only came in because I was curious what was going on in here," Teegan replied, adding under her breath as she turned to go, "I'll leave you to your chess games and the nerds playing here!"

April tried not to show how Teegan's comments hurt. "Hi Gabe," she said quietly, "Glad you could come."

"Yeah, almost didn't make it today. Got stuck when I couldn't open one of the doors on the way, but thankfully Teegan opened it for me."

"Well, next time I'll plan on checking in with you and giving you a hand if you need it," April said, rather surprised that Teegan had noticed and helped Gabe. She wondered whether perhaps Teegan was nicer than her comments implied.

Gabe smiled. "Thank you, April."

"Okay everyone, please take your seats as we are ready to get started," Cathy said. Once the room was quiet, she continued, "First, I want to welcome the young students visiting from the local elementary and middle schools. Please give them a warm welcome as they are joining us today to prepare for the upcoming competitions as well!"

The high school chess club members clapped loudly. "I assume you're all here because there is a big opportunity coming up. At the chess tournaments coming up, any player scoring 3 or more wins will qualify and move on to the state championships. In addition, thanks to a private donor, besides the recognition that comes with winning the champion's trophy, first place in this year's state championships includes a pretty amazing $5,000 scholarship to help the winner attend the college of their choice!"

April smiled to herself. She was starting to believe that maybe she could earn the scholarship.

"Ok, here's what you'll need to know in order to do well at the qualifier, as well as the district tournament," the coach announced. "You must remember the basic rules starting with First Touch: If you touch a piece, you must move it – so take your time and think with your head, not with your hands!"

"In fact, if you have a habit of touching pieces, just sit on your hands until you're ready to move! It'll help keep your hands warm," he joked.

"Second, tournament rules require players to be quiet during the games – no talking is permitted other than to say things like 'Check' or 'Checkmate.'"

The chess coach went on through each rule printed on the papers, explaining what they were and giving tips on how to achieve their best in the tournament.

"Now, let's move into practice time – we'll pretend we're competing in the tournament – imagine that you are playing your first game there. Please find a partner, sit down at the chessboards, and wait for the signal to begin."

April sat at her board waiting for someone to play with. She was happy when one of the elementary students she recognized as a classmate of Max's came over and sat down across from her. He appeared to be rather timid, and as he sat down across from April he bumped the table, knocking over a couple of pieces. April noticed that when he set the pieces back up, he placed a couple pieces on the wrong squares.

April smiled kindly as she corrected his mistake by reaching over to switch the king and queen. "It's easy to mix up. Just remember, the queen sits on her own color – light-colored queen goes on the light-colored square."

"Thank you," he replied, not looking up from the board.

"Ok, remember to shake hands before and after every game, be a good sport, and begin your games!" the coach called out.

April shook hands with her opponent and started the game confidently. She knew just what to do, as she had been learning from the online program.

She moved her pawns to the middle of the board, brought out her knights and bishops and then castled her king.

Once she had moved all the pieces on her back rank, bringing each of the pieces into the game, she started to wonder what to do next, but still felt very confident as her opponent seemed to be having even more difficulty figuring out what to do.

She moved forward and captured a dark bishop, which seemed

to surprise her opponent – and she saw an opportunity to take a few more undefended pieces. Her confidence swelled, and she was about to advance a pawn all the way to the other side of the board – which would promote into another piece – when her opponent moved his queen across the board, taking the pawn right in front of her king, and said "Checkmate!"

April was shocked! She looked carefully – but sure enough, her king could not capture the queen because it was supported by a rook – she hadn't noticed her opponent lining up his pieces at her king. How could she lose to someone so young who didn't even know how to correctly set up the chess pieces? She tried to fight back the tears.

"I told you! Girls can't play chess!" Max's comment made her jump. He was standing beside her looking at the chessboard, apparently already having finished his own game. Not able to hold her feelings in anymore, April jumped up and ran out of the room and down the hallway, the tears now coming freely, blinding her so she nearly bumped into someone coming out of the staff room. "April, what's the matter? Come with me." Cathy gently laid her hand on April's shoulder and guided her to a seat in a quiet corner.

"I can't do it! I'm just not good at chess!" April said, tears pouring down her cheeks.

Cathy just listened, letting April finish crying. When April had quieted down, she said gently, "Tell me – what happened?"

April mentioned everything that had happened in the chess club session, how there were hardly any girls, and how she had even been checkmated by a classmate of Max's who had apparently not even known how to correctly set up the chess pieces.

When April finished telling her story, Cathy appeared to be musing a little. Then she spoke quietly, "Let me understand a bit more – you said that you felt you were winning the game at one point?"

"Yes," April replied. "I was ahead by several pieces, and I was about to get a new queen by promoting my pawn."

"So, at that point," Cathy continued, "do you recall what you were thinking?"

April thought for a minute. "I was thinking about winning. I was already imagining myself winning the tournament and the scholarship."

"Yes," Cathy replied, "and then, while dreaming of the future, what happened to the present?"

"I didn't see what he was doing. He lined up his queen and rook and checkmated my king," April replied in a low voice. The tears nearly came again.

"Exactly," Cathy replied, "that's what I was suspecting. You see, what has happened is that you have just experienced a very painful lesson, but a very valuable one which we can put into a single word: respect."

"Respect?" April repeated the word. "I don't know what you mean. Are you saying I was disrespectful?"

"No, that is not what I meant," Cathy replied. "Here I'm using the word respect to mean something a bit different.

"Let's start with an aspect of respect that is perhaps simple to understand. When you were listening to the coach explain the rules, would you say that you showed respect to him?"

"Yes," replied April.

"So how did you show respect to him?" Cathy asked.

April thought for a bit. "Let me see. I didn't interrupt him, and I raised my hand to ask a question then waited for him to give me permission before asking… and…," She thought hard. "I guess perhaps I showed respect by listening carefully?"

"Well said," Cathy said and smiled warmly. "You see, you showed respect through your actions, showing that you placed a high value on the teacher and his knowledge. Respect includes the aspect of valuing someone. Additionally, there is also an aspect of humility included with respect: the attitude of 'there's something

I can learn from this person,' instead of an attitude of pride or 'know-it-all.'"

"Oh, I think I'm starting to understand," April said. "I was thinking that I was winning, so I started to think that I would automatically win the game because I knew I had a very good position. Then because I didn't respect my opponent's knowledge, I became careless and forgot to look at what he could still do!"

"Yes," Cathy smiled, "that's correct – and the result? A painful loss. However, just keep this in mind: a dream like the one you have is not an easy journey. Many times the greater the dream, the greater the pain involved, but in those moments of pain often are some of the best lessons."

Cathy continued. "Before we move forward though, there is just a little more I would like to share about respect. Did you know that you can also show respect towards objects, not just people?"

Seeing April's puzzled look, Cathy added, "Remember that respect involves showing value for someone? You can also show respect for things by showing you value them. For example, when you play chess, what would happen if when you were done, you left the chessboard and pieces out on the table without putting them away?"

"Well, a piece might become lost," April replied.

"Exactly, or, when you put them away, if you don't treat them carefully, what might happen?" Cathy continued.

"A piece could chip or break."

"Yes, and then how valuable would the chess set be with a missing or broken piece?" Cathy asked.

"Not very," April replied. She was quiet for a minute as suddenly images of her bedroom had come to mind, and the many times she had just tossed her clothes in a pile or left them bundled up and how they became wrinkled, and of the torn pages in her books that happened all too frequently. Quietly she resolved to show respect to her things as well as to people.

"Well, I think you have had a very good lesson today." Cathy stood up as she spoke. "I'm really proud of you and how you are making progress."

As they walked out together, Cathy asked with a little smile, "So, are you still going to give up?"

April replied with a smile as well. "No indeed! I'm going to do my best, and anytime I'm winning in the future, I'll simply continue looking carefully for the best move, showing respect for all my opponents."

"Very good," said Cathy. "Are you ready to move forward and learn the next fundamental life skill? One that will help you greatly improve your chess skills?"

"Yes!" said April eagerly, "What is it?"

"It's too late to cover it today," Cathy replied. "However, it's simply a way that you can actually win when you lose."

"Win when I lose? I don't understand. What do you mean?" April replied with a puzzled look.

Cathy smiled and waved goodbye. "I'll give you some time to think about it."

As April returned home that night, she felt her confidence returning. She felt sure that in the future she would show respect to her opponents; plus, she was excited to find ways she could show more respect to her family as well as to her personal belongings. On top of that, April was eager to figure out what Cathy meant by saying "win when you lose." Perhaps she could seek out Gabe the next day and ask him if he knew what it meant.

CHAPTER 8

APRIL AWOKE THE next morning with a sore throat, which made it rather difficult for her to swallow. She got up anyway, dressed, and made her way to the kitchen. She wasn't about to miss a chance to find out just what the life skill was that could greatly improve her chess skills.

She had no appetite but started on her breakfast anyway, wincing a little as she swallowed because of the pain in her throat.

"What's the matter, April? Are you not feeling well?" Sara asked, noticing how April was only picking at her food.

"My throat hurts," April said. "But I'm ok – I don't want to miss school today."

April was usually quite happy to miss a day of school and stay home – now she was trying to make sure she went to school!

"I'm sorry," Sara replied kindly, "but if you are sick, you don't want to get the others at school sick, would you?"

"No, that wouldn't be good," April said slowly, feeling disappointed to miss school but also thinking how bad it would be if Gabe got a sore throat.

"I could ask one of the neighbors to come check in to see if you need anything while I'm gone. I'm sorry I can't stay home myself," Sara said, picking up her keys and heading for the door.

"That's ok, no need to do that. I'll be fine," April replied.

After her family left, April decided she might as well use the time alone as an opportunity to practice her chess. She went to the computer to log on but found the internet was down. She tried to reboot it a few times but to no avail. She sighed and decided to try again later, then turned off the computer and slowly wandered back to her bedroom.

As she sat on her bed wondering what she could do, her eyes fell on the box containing the robot kit that Max had opened without permission. On the packaging, it read "Explore! Discover! DREAM BIG! For this Robot can extend your reach, expand your abilities, and do things you thought impossible before!" She decided to take a look and carried the box to her desk.

As April picked up the paper instructions, she read, "What you have in your hands is no ordinary toy. This is a Robotic Arm limited only by your imagination! It can do many things, and the real question is, what is the DREAM that you want to achieve? What can YOU do with this Robot?"

The words resonated with her, and she started looking more closely at the parts and wondering how the robot could help her. She didn't think there was a way, but maybe it was possible?

April followed the instructions to assemble the Robotic Arm, intrigued especially by a few rather fascinating parts with multiple joints that she correctly guessed functioned similarly to fingers and a hand. It wasn't long before most of the pieces were in position.

When April came to the controller for the Robotic Arm, there was a switch to turn it on and a variety of buttons. She turned the switch on and read on the small display, "ready for programming." She was puzzled a bit so looked carefully at the directions.

Steps to program your Robot:

Once you have assembled all of the parts, connect the robot via the adapter to a computer. Next, visit the robotic arm website to download the most recent software programming package. Next, follow the software instructions to program your robotic arm.

Note: this robotic arm can move in any direction and hold, pick up, or move nearly anything within its range. Finally, remember you are limited only by your imagination!

April looked back in the box and found the small cable she had missed before. She carried the robotic arm to the computer and turned the computer on, hoping the internet was working now. Yes, it was!

Quickly finding the robotic arm website, April clicked on the button to download the software.

Once it was finished installing, she opened the program. There was a sample program which April decided to try out.

She clicked on the Install button. Once the program had finished installing, she unplugged the robotic arm from the computer, used the straps to attach the robot to her arm, and then tested the controls to try it out. It took a bit to get used to, but once she got the hang of it, it was really fun to pick up items using the robot.

After a while, April went back to the software to explore the programs further and learned about the 'eye' on the robot that could be programmed to recognize various items and respond accordingly. There was even a 'voice recognition' component that allowed you to program some voice commands to which the robot would respond!

April found the program increasingly fascinating, and she started looking around for various items to try to program the robot to pick up. She spied a knight from Max's chess set lying on the floor! With some trial and error, she was able to make the robot pick up the piece and set it on the board.

Suddenly a thought flashed into her mind. *I wonder if Gabe... imagine if this robotic arm could work for Gabe! Maybe...just maybe if it was programmed well, he could use it to move the chess pieces more easily. Maybe even pick up pieces off the floor when they fall...maybe he could even do more things for himself like eating! April was growing more excited with every minute.*

Time flew by, and before she knew it, the school bus had pulled up and shortly afterward Max came bursting through the door.

Max dropped his backpack in the doorway – and paused as he saw the Robot strapped to April's arm. "Nice!" he said. "Does it work? Can I try it?"

"Watch this," April said, as she rather expertly maneuvered the Robotic Arm to reach out and pick up a chess piece, then move it. "Wow! That's awesome!" Max was fascinated with the robotic arm. "Let me try?"

April strapped the robot onto Max's arm and helped him learn the various buttons. It didn't take long before he also was able to pick things up with the robot.

After some more time practicing with the robot, April said, "Everyone is going to be home soon. Let's put this away for now." That night, once again, April had a hard time falling to sleep.

Thoughts of the robot possibly helping Gabe to be able to do so many of the things that he couldn't do easily now kept her mind going, as she puzzled over how she could perhaps make it work. Then she thought of Michael – he was president of the robotics club. *Maybe I'll just ask and see if he has some ideas.* With this thought, she finally fell asleep, dreaming of robots playing in chess tournaments.

CHAPTER 9

APRIL SPENT EVERY minute she could spare continuing her chess studies in the online platform, as well as practicing with Gabe, Max, and other members of the chess club.

The state qualifying tournament was coming soon, and she wanted to be ready!

When April told her parents that she would like to play in the chess tournament, they were more than a little surprised.

"You know how to play chess? When did you learn?" They asked several questions, quite puzzled not just by her knowledge of playing chess but also her determination to play in the tournament. April was glad that her parents gave their approval – and secretly glad when it became apparent that neither of her parents would be able to come to the event, both having prior commitments for work. April really didn't want them to be there for her first attempt at qualifying for state. She was even happier that neither of them asked her why she was so determined to play – she was not ready yet to share her goal to win the chess scholarship.

The day of the tournament came all too fast. April hoped she was ready. She had started to win more of her practice games; she had studied diligently, and she had tried to focus on maintaining a 'Can-Do Attitude.' Still, she was considerably nervous about competing in an actual tournament.

As she walked into the school's multi-purpose room where the tournament was to be held, April was glad to see Cathy and ran up to her to say good morning.

"Good morning, April!" Cathy smiled brightly, and then added, "You feel ready to qualify for state?"

April nodded, although she felt a bit overwhelmed. There were many people already there, as the event drew competitors from several neighboring schools. Many of them were also striving to qualify for the state championships.

April was glad to notice that she wasn't the only girl at this event, though there was what appeared to be about a ten-to-one ratio of boys to girls.

April saw Gabe and ran over to say good morning to him. She nearly mentioned the Robotic Arm to him but managed to catch herself before saying anything. Instead, she asked, "Are you excited to compete again?"

"Yes," he replied. "Even more, I'm quite excited to meet the master!"

April was curious. "The master? What do you mean?"

"See that man over there? The one talking to the chess club coach?" Gabe answered.

April followed his look and saw a professional-looking man in a sports jacket with slacks and dress shirt. He was listening intently to the chess club coach who April figured, based on where he looked, must be discussing various students from the club.

"Who is he?" April asked.

"He's a national master in chess" Gabe replied. "He's quite skilled. I've heard he can even play chess blindfolded against several opponents at once! Cathy said he was going to be here, and I would love to ask him some questions about my chess openings."

April wasn't sure still what 'master' meant in the context of chess – but she assumed it meant he must be very good at playing chess. She thought too that it would be neat to meet him, though she was a little shy about going up to him on her own.

Opening announcements were made, and then it was time for the tournament to begin.

In April's first game, she was quite pleased to follow her plan of bringing out her pieces, then aiming them at one of the pawns in front of her opponent's king, which was defended only by the king. Her opponent missed what she was planning, and April was able to checkmate him fairly quickly.

In her next game, April played another girl who was also playing in her first tournament. Once again, April was able to find a checkmate.

Her confidence rose, and even after losing her third game in a close match, she still felt optimistic. The fourth game, however, was a bit of a surprise to her. April's opponent seemed to see every threat she made, countered with his own attack, and, before April knew it, her opponent had April's king trapped.

April's confidence was shaken, but talking with Gabe before the final game helped as Gabe reminded her that it only takes three wins out of five games to qualify for the state championships. As the time came closer for the start of the final round, she was very excited and started dreaming about going on to the state championships and what it would be like to surprise her parents.

It was not to be! April's opponent seemed to be in control right from the start, playing a couple moves April had not seen before, which confused her. The game was over in less than 15 minutes, her king checkmated.

April didn't know what had happened and barely remembered to shake hands after the game. She felt dazed – and her dreams seemed to once again come crashing down around her. She walked out of the tournament playing room still bewildered. She had been so sure that she would qualify – yet it hadn't happened. Doubt crept in. Could she really do this? Could she really play chess?

Cathy was surprised to see April come out of the tournament room so soon. She was about to ask, "Are you done?" when she saw the look on April's face and knew the answer. Instead, she just walked up to April and put her arm around her shoulders.

After about a minute, Cathy said, "You know, I'm really proud of you. You just finished your first chess tournament, a state qualifying tournament at that. You even won a couple of games! Don't worry about not qualifying for state – there will be more opportunities. You've really made great progress already. Just think back to when you first met Gabe! Did you ever think you would be able to play in a chess tournament, let alone win some games?"

April thought about it for a minute and brightened up a little. "You're right! I was so disappointed about not qualifying – I nearly forgot to see how far I've come already! Thank you for reminding me."

Cathy continued, "There's someone I would like you to meet." By now April had learned that when Cathy said this, she usually had something very important that she wanted April to learn. "Who is it?" April asked.

"Here, just come with me," Cathy said.

Cathy led the way to a room they called the 'skittles room,' where participants would typically spend time between rounds. She led April to a couple of comfortable chairs and said, "Why don't you wait here – I'll be right back."

In just a couple of minutes, Cathy returned with the chess master following her!

"Here's the young lady I mentioned to you," Cathy said to the master, then turned to April. "April, I would like you to meet our special guest at today's tournament, Eduardo. I need to take care of a few things, so I'll be back in a little while."

"Nice to meet you, April! Do you mind if I ask what grade you are in?" Eduardo had a kind voice.

"I'm a sophomore," April replied, rather shyly. She had to find out though, "Are you the best chess player in the world?"

"Oh no, not even close," he laughed lightly. "Would you like to learn about what it takes to become a chess master?"

"Oh yes, please!" April replied eagerly, curiosity taking over. "I'll be happy to share, but let me first ask a few questions,"

Eduardo said. "How long have you been playing chess?"

"About two months."

"Is it correct that this is your first tournament?" he continued. "Yes," April answered.

"Congratulations on finishing your first tournament! That's already a great accomplishment. Do you know what a chess rating is?" he continued.

April shook her head, "No, not really. I remember Cathy saying that a chess rating is a way to measure progress in chess, but I don't know how it works."

"A chess rating is simply a number that you earn by playing chess games in rated tournaments," Eduardo said. "A person who knows how the chess pieces move, but not much more than that, typically starts out with a rating of about 400. As you win games, your rating goes up, and as you lose games, your rating goes down."

Eduardo continued, "Earning a rating of 1000 typically means the player knows some important basic concepts; a rating of 1400 means the person has expanded their knowledge and skills quite a bit further; 1800 means the person has already reached the upper levels of players in the country; and passing 2200 means the person has achieved what is necessary to be considered a master in chess."

"Are there many masters in chess?" April asked.

"No, it's actually quite rare," he replied. "In fact, it's about as rare for someone to earn a Ph.D. as it is to become a master. When I achieved the master level, I was ranked in the top 15 players in the state, and as a teenager, among my age group, I was also ranked in the top 20 in the whole country. Being a master usually means being in the top 1% to 2% of all chess players."

"What's the highest someone can go?" April asked.

"Well, the world champion is usually rated over 2800, but no one has reached 3000 yet!" he replied.

April wanted to ask another question but was a little hesitant. Eduardo noticed that she paused, waited a couple of moments, and when she still didn't speak, said, "Is there something else you would like to ask?"

April was rather startled that he had apparently recognized that she wanted to ask another question.

"Well, yes..." she said hesitantly, and then grew a bit bolder. "I was wondering – what rating would it take to win the state championships for my grade?"

"April," he said kindly, "tell me please – why is it so important to you to win the state championships when you have just begun playing chess?"

"Well, you see," April struggled to keep her voice steady, "I really want to go to college. My Dad didn't get the promotion at work that he was expecting; my mom is a school teacher – they work really hard but don't have enough money for me to go to college. My brother won a scholarship, so he's able to go, but for me – I've not really been good at anything...," she said, her voice trailing off.

"If you've felt as if you couldn't succeed in other things, what gave you enough confidence to believe that you could succeed with chess?" he asked.

"Gabe," April simply replied.

"Gabe?" Eduardo repeated, "I'm not sure I understand."

"You see, one day Cathy invited me to meet someone," April replied, "and she took me to see Gabe. He has no arms or legs – well, he has just a small stump of a foot – and he plays chess! Gabe taught me how to play, and, well, I guess if someone like him can play chess – and not only play chess – he's won a tournament and a scholarship, I just felt I should be able to do it too!" Her voice strengthened as she went on, and she finished telling the story of how she had learned not only chess but the 'Can-Do Attitude' from Gabe.

Eduardo was quiet for a moment and then spoke. "So, you asked what rating it takes to win the state championships."

April nodded.

Eduardo said, "Let me tell you a story. I played in my first National Championship tournament when I had just turned thirteen. This was a tournament that was open to all ages, not just school ages. I had been studying intensively for some time, so my playing strength was probably about 1600 at the time even though I had not played in enough events to have my rating catch up. My Dad gave me some wise advice before that tournament. He had noticed that if I saw someone's rating, I could be intimidated by a high-rated opponent, and a bit overconfident if facing a low-rated opponent, so he suggested to me that instead of looking at ratings, I simply play the game with whomever I was paired with each round, and only after each game find out their rating."

As other participants finishing their games entered the skittles room, they noticed the chess master talking with April and gathered around, eager to hear what he was saying.

Eduardo continued his story, "My dad said to me, 'Why don't you do your best to forget about who is sitting across the board from you? Focus only on the chess pieces on the board – that's what you are playing with. Think of it like this: Every turn you have a chess puzzle to solve and think over carefully as to how to find the answer. Don't waste any time thinking about your opponent's rating or even about winning – that's simply wasted energy. Think only about what is happening on the board and take your time to look for the BEST move you can find. Then, whatever happens, happens.'

"In this tournament, I carefully followed my Dad's advice, and one round I found myself sitting across from a man who looked rather intimidating. He had a foreign-sounding name and appeared to be close to my Dad's age. Well, I determined to just do my best on the board and not think at all about him. I even used my hands to shield my eyes from seeing him to focus just on the position!

"I was playing the dark pieces, and my opponent moved quickly, developing his pieces and then launching a powerful attack against my castled king. I was focused on defending when at one point he said quietly, almost as if he was talking to himself, 'I'm going to checkmate the king soon.'"

It was as if Eduardo was reliving the moment, and April along with the other players now surrounding them found themselves holding their breath, waiting to find out what happened.

He continued, "When my opponent made that comment, my first thought was 'uh-oh, did I miss something?' But then right away I remembered my dad's advice about simply focusing on the chess pieces on the board and took my time to think very carefully. Suddenly I saw something I could do! It was difficult to discover, but I found a way to trade off the best attackers. Then even though my king was in danger, I was able to find a way to get the king to safety and along the way even win one of my opponent's pawns.

"It took me a long time to figure this out, but it worked! I survived the attack, and a short time later was able to build my own attack against his king and checkmated him!"

Several of those listening clapped their hands. April let out a long breath and smiled. "You must have been really excited to win that game!"

"Yes, indeed I was," Eduardo replied. "After the game, I asked my opponent what his rating was, as I was curious.

" 'I'm rated 2200,' my opponent replied.

"I looked at him not comprehending what I had just heard, but as it sunk in, suddenly my knees started to shake and knock against each other. I had just defeated my first MASTER level opponent! I thanked him for the game, and then went to find my Dad and tell him about the game, still not believing that I had actually defeated a master in my first national tournament!"

Eduardo paused in his story and looked around at the audience listening. "What do you think would have happened if I had known he was a master before the game started?"

"You probably would have been afraid and lost?" one of the students suggested.

"Exactly," Eduardo replied. "I probably would have been too distracted by how high his rating was and about my playing a master for the first time in my life, and because of that probably would not have played as well as I did. Perhaps my opponent had looked at my rating and assumed that because it was low, the game would be easy for him to win. Either way, I had just defeated a master for the first time, and this gave me tremendous confidence, as well as made me realize that I really could become a master someday myself.

"So, April," Eduardo smiled, "let me ask you – what rating do you think it takes to win the state championships?"

April also smiled. "I guess that any rating is good enough to win the state championships if I just focus on playing the best moves and have a Can-Do Attitude?"

"Yes," he replied, "that is certainly true! However, attitude alone is not enough; because of course it's important to have knowledge and skill as well. It's just that if we ever let fear of someone or something come into our minds, it will block our ability to apply what we have learned. You see, a chess rating simply is a means of showing how someone has played in the past – it is no guarantee of how someone will play in a specific game.

"Okay, what do you think, April – do you still want to win the state championships?"

"Oh yes, more than ever!" April replied. "I think I understand more about attitude and rating now. But what can I do to get the skills and knowledge? I've been learning from the online platform using the videos, training activities, and puzzles plus I've been playing practice games – but I'm not sure if that's good enough. What else can I do?" April looked at Eduardo eagerly.

"You're doing many of the right things to improve; practicing, adding knowledge, competing – those are all good!" he replied. "Let me give you just two more suggestions for now that you can consider following. Again, these come from my own experience, and indeed can be applied by all of you." He looked around at the group of chess players listening intently.

"So, April, what was your score in today's tournament?" he asked.

"I won two and then lost three," April replied. "I would disagree with you," Eduardo replied.

Now April was really puzzled. "What do you mean? I checkmated the first two games, and my king was checkmated the last three."

Eduardo smiled. "Well, it comes down to another mindset, meaning how you think about something. If all you are looking at is the game, then yes, you can say you won or lost – but was your goal simply to win a game? What was your goal?"

"I wanted to qualify for state," April replied.

"Yes, I understand," he replied, "but didn't you say that your real goal is to win the scholarship?"

"Well yes," April slowly replied, "and I need to qualify for the state championships in order to play in it, and I need to win three games in order to qualify for state."

"Very true," Eduardo said. "However, what can you control? Can you really control the outcome of a game? Or of the tournament? Isn't it rather dependent on your finding better moves than your opponent?" He looked around at the group as he spoke.

Heads nodded as April replied hesitantly, "I suppose so," still puzzled at what Eduardo meant.

"You see," Eduardo continued slowly, striving to help April understand. "Because you can only control your actions, not anyone else's actions, and because you cannot control the outcomes – then really the only thing that you can do to help you potentially win the scholarship is what?"

"Perhaps increase my knowledge and skill in chess?" April answered hesitantly.

"Yes," Eduardo replied. "You are doing that with the online play, and you are ALSO doing that when you play in any competition. You put into practice what you have been learning. Here's one of my secrets: EVERY single game I play is a chance to increase my knowledge by LEARNING something from my opponent. You see, instead of win or lose, my attitude is that I can Win, Draw (if neither side can win), or LEARN!

"It was after winning against that master in my first national championships, that I had a new dream to become a master myself one day. Every single game I played after that, I was striving to learn something new, striving to build my knowledge and the skills essential to becoming a master. Whether I won a game or not, I no longer saw it as losing, since it was helping me learn what I needed to achieve my dream.

"Because of this mindset," Eduardo continued, "I went from my first rated game to achieving the master level in fewer than three hundred fifty rated games, when for many masters it would not be unusual to take closer to one thousand rated games to get there, if not more."

April was quiet for a minute as the thought of losing being 'learning' sunk in. She realized now that this must have been what Cathy meant when she had said that you could turn losing into winning.

Another student spoke up, "But how did you learn from each game? I can't even remember what happened in my last game!"

Eduardo smiled again. "Remember the letters and numbers used to name every square on the board? If you form a habit of writing down all your moves in a chess game as you play it, then you will have a record of what you have played and can learn from it.

"When I was young, I made it a habit to write down all my

moves; in fact, I still have the records from my earliest games. I could even show you the record of that game against my first master! After every tournament game I would ask my opponent, especially if I had just lost, if they would be willing to review the game with me and see if we could figure out ways to improve. Reviewing these games helped me learn much as I listened to what my opponent had been thinking about in the game. I started to understand why certain moves were played, and what the ideas were. I learned in many cases far more when I lost a game and then listened to my opponent explain the plans/ideas they had, than if I had won a game. This is why I've come to call this mindset simply 'Win, Draw, or Learn!'"

"The tournament is finished!" Cathy said, entering the room. She walked over to Eduardo and spoke to him: "We would appreciate it if you would be willing to say a few things to all the participants as well as hand out the awards. I think there are quite a few players who would love to get your autograph if there is time afterward."

"I'll be happy to do so," Eduardo replied, standing up and reaching out his hand to April.

"Thank you for helping me learn how to win when I lose," April said and smiled as she shook hands. "I believe I can win the championships and maybe even become a master also someday."

He smiled, "I'm sure you can, April. Just one more thing," he spoke slowly and very clearly, "Win, Draw, Learn works in chess – and it also works in life. Just because you've perhaps lost in other areas, doesn't mean you can't achieve. You really CAN – what matters is your mindset."

The group surrounding the chess master applauded and started moving towards the main room where the awards would be given.

"Did you enjoy meeting Eduardo?" Cathy asked with a smile as the room emptied.

"Did I? That was amazing! He was so nice too!" April replied.

"Thank you for giving me the opportunity to learn about the mindset of success. I'm going to become a master someday," she added quietly.

"I believe it – I'm sure you can," Cathy replied. "There is another state qualifying chess tournament – quite a large one as it's open to the whole district and will be held at the largest high school in the district. It 's called the Last Chance Qualifier as that is the last date on which a person can qualify to compete in the championships. What do you think?"

"I'm going to qualify," April replied quietly. "I've got much to learn, but I know what I can do. I can focus on improving my knowledge and learning from every game. I'll be ready."

"I believe you will be ready," Cathy replied, then continued, "There are, however, a few more people I would like you to meet before that tournament. I'll see what I can do to make this happen."

As they walked back to the tournament room, April wondered to herself who Cathy was planning to have her meet. Even more, she wondered what she would be learning from meeting these people.

As April reflected on her meeting with Eduardo, she suddenly thought of something. She hurried off trying to find her last round opponent – she wanted to ask him to review the game with her, hoping she could apply "Win, Draw, Learn" to her most recent game.

CHAPTER 10

AS THE DAYS passed, April continued to work on her chess studies, practicing every chance she could, writing down her moves even in practice games with Gabe and other members of the chess club. She embraced the Win, Draw, Learn mindset, and loved to ask every person she competed with questions about the moves they played as she worked hard to improve from every game.

About a week after the tournament, April was thinking about the chess master Eduardo again as she arrived at school and started heading to her classroom when a familiar voice interrupted her thoughts. "Playing so much chess these days you don't know where you're going?" Teegan said teasingly. April suddenly realized that she was going the opposite direction that all the other students were headed. Then she remembered – today was the all-school assembly and there was a special guest, a magician!

"I just forgot today was the assembly," April said to Teegan as she turned around and followed the crowd into the large room. She wished that Teegan would say nicer things. She wasn't sure whether Teegan was trying to be mean or just didn't realize how her words affected others. As usual, April decided to say nothing about it for now and quietly found a seat.

There was a greater sense of anticipation than usual in the

school assembly. The magician coming had been the talk of the school for quite some time – apparently, he had attended this very high school!

The assembly quieted down when the principal of the school walked on stage with mic in hand. "Friends, students, teachers, and parents – it is with great pleasure that I introduce today a very special guest; one who attended school right here and who has discovered his talent and developed it. From humble beginnings, this gentleman devoted himself to developing his talent; he worked hard and won many prizes for his abilities. He has represented the United States in international magician competitions and shows. Recently he has opened his own theatre in the Bahamas, where he performs regularly and has been ranked as the #1 show by popular tourist websites. Please help me welcome our special guest, Keanu!"

The crowd clapped loudly as from behind a curtain on stage stepped the magician. April was surprised at how young he appeared – she had imagined magicians as being old. Before she could get over her surprise, the show began.

Keanu was wearing a flowing black overcoat that matched his pitch-black, perfectly-styled hair.

It was quickly obvious that this was no ordinary magician. Keanu put on a show involving intricate dance steps, the music fitting each act, and every detail was choreographed beautifully as he flowed easily from one illusion to another.

April was amazed at how Keanu made a deck of cards appear out of nowhere – and then suddenly the cards morphed into giant cards, at least 6 inches long. She couldn't figure out how he possibly had the cards hidden. His hands really didn't appear large enough to hide the large cards.

The audience cheered loudly as he even caused a chair on stage to float up off the stage without anyone touching it!

Keanu bowed and disappeared behind the black curtain backdrop on stage. The music changed to a quieter, riveting melody as Keanu emerged with a flat cardboard box under his arm. The audience was quiet, wondering what was going to happen. He walked over to a bare, four-legged table. It was obvious that nothing could be hidden at the table, as there was no tablecloth and you could see under the table to where he stood.

Keanu turned the cardboard box both ways so the audience could see it was flat. Then, as he slowly unfolded the box, he started speaking in a lower voice, giving the impression that he had a serious message. "Friends, sometimes things in life are not as they appear to be, and what matters is not what you see – but what you believe can be. Sometimes life itself can appear as empty as this cardboard box. But even if you feel that you have nothing, focus not on what you do not have, but on what CAN BE. Believe – and not just believe – take action to prepare. You see, just as this cardboard box is opening so that it may be filled, preparation is key. You may think, what's the point of preparing an empty box? Well, those who do not prepare, do not receive – but if you prepare, you may indeed receive!"

With that, Keanu reached down into the box and lifted out what looked like a large chess piece – yes, a knight! As the audience gasped in surprise, he took the knight and walked down off the stage among the audience, handing it to several audience members to inspect. When she had the opportunity, April held the large chess piece with wonder – she saw that it was made of hard plastic, lightweight, and the bottom part could be screwed on or off – something that showed her it was not a piece that was collapsible. After examining it closely, she handed the large chess piece back to Keanu, who was waiting to retrieve the knight. As he walked back on stage, he continued, "Friends, when you start with what feels like nothing, remember that what matters is what is inside of you, not what is outside."

As Keanu slowly placed the giant chess knight back inside the cardboard box, he added, "Be very careful, because if you believe that you have nothing inside you – it may indeed come true!" As he said these words, he made a swift movement and collapsed the cardboard box with a loud THUMP! The box was again flat with no chess piece to be seen anywhere!!

Keanu picked up the flat box, tucking it under his arm and turning around both ways so the audience could see there was no chess piece hidden and walked behind the curtain. The audience was so stunned by the surprise ending as well as the depth of the message Keanu had shared, that they were quiet for a few seconds, and then they all burst out in applause and cheers.

Keanu came back on stage and bowed. "Thank you for coming!" he said. "It is my hope that each one of you will recognize that the box is representative of each of us and that within are potentially many wonderful, surprising things. It is as full (or empty) as you think it is."

As the audience filed out, April sat thinking deeply about the message Keanu had shared. It struck home to her as she remembered thinking about how she had nothing, and how through meeting Gabe and learning chess, she had discovered she did indeed have the ability to learn something that at first had seemed impossible for her. She started to wonder about the magician. Did he always know that he could be a magician? I wonder how he became so good.

"Would you like to find out?"

April realized with a start that she must have been speaking her thoughts out loud, as Cathy stood there smiling.

"Why, yes, I would indeed but I'm already nearly late for class," April replied quickly, standing up.

"Don't worry about class, April. I'll be happy to let your teacher know why you'll be arriving late – I'm sure it will be fine considering this special opportunity. Come with me." Cathy led the way to the stage where the magician was signing a few autographs for the remaining guests. As he finished, Keanu looked up and saw Cathy and April approaching.

"Thank you for inviting me back here, Cathy. It's certainly been a pleasure to come and be able to give back a little," Keanu said with a smile.

He turned to April. "Hi, I'm Keanu! What's your name?" "April," she replied. "That was amazing! How did you become so good at being a magician?"

Keanu looked at Cathy who smiled, nodded, and then asked, "Do you still have a little time?"

"Yes, I'll be happy to take some time," Keanu replied.

"April," he said, "Cathy mentioned to me that there was someone she thought could benefit from my story. I take it she meant you – would you like to hear my story?"

"Yes, I would love that!" April replied eagerly.

"Here, let's sit down over here." Keanu indicated a couple chairs still in the room. "My assistant will be fine putting things away for a bit, so we have a few minutes."

April sat down on the edge of her seat, eager to hear Keanu's story.

"Well," he began, "I was once a student just getting along. Not that great in anything, not sure what I wanted to do, just very uncertain about the future.

"However, that all changed after I met Cathy. She seemed to notice that I was drifting, and she introduced me to Eduardo the chess master, with whom I learned to play chess – and not only play chess – but also to set some challenging goals."

"What was your goal in chess?" April asked eagerly.

"I really wanted to win our state's junior championships while still in high school," Keanu replied.

"So what happened? What did you do? Did you win it?" April asked.

Keanu continued, "When I shared this goal with Eduardo, he paused, looked at me for what seemed quite a long time, and then said very slowly to me, 'Keanu, do you REALLY want to become the state junior chess champion? Or is it just a wish and a dream?'

"I thought carefully and replied, 'I'm not sure I can do it, but I REALLY want to achieve this. Will you help me?'

"Eduardo said to me, 'How about we first do the following: While this is a great goal to have, and I do believe it is achievable, let's first lay out a plan for what it would take to achieve the goal. Then you can decide if you are willing to commit to the effort it takes to achieve that plan. Sound good?'

"I nodded.

"He proceeded to lay out a plan of what it would take for me to achieve the playing strength necessary to have a good chance at winning the tournament. He told me which chess books he would recommend I study and events I needed to play in order to practice and hone my chess skills. When we looked at the timeline, it appeared that I would need to put in about twelve hours each week as the minimum to achieve the goal. When he had finished going through the plan with me, he looked at me for a minute, just quietly watching me as I thought about what he had laid out as necessary to achieve the goal.

"Then he continued, 'Keanu, I cannot do this for you. Based on my experience, I've laid out what I think it would take to help you gain the skill necessary to have a good chance at achieving your goal. The real question is; how important is this goal to you? Are you willing to put in the effort it will take to have a chance at succeeding in your goal?'

"I thought that over carefully, and then I said, 'Yes, I'm willing to commit to the effort. I really want to achieve this – I've never been a champion – I really want to succeed in this!'"

As April listened to Keanu tell his story, she leaned forward, listening intently. She felt drawn into his story as it resonated with how she was feeling – how she so desperately wanted to accomplish her own dream.

Keanu continued, "The master replied slowly, looking directly at me, 'I'm happy to hear you say this. I believe you can! It's what's inside of you that matters. Just know that there will be difficulties along the way, that you will feel like quitting many times, and that in those times it is crucial to first remember WHY you are committed to the effort – to remember your dream of becoming champion. Then simply focus on taking the next step spelled out in the plan to fulfill your dream. Do not measure your success by how you feel about your results in your practice games. Trust me in this, and simply focus on controlling what you can control – your effort at studying and striving to do your best in every practice time, always putting in at least the amount of effort that we laid out in the plan – more when you can. Are you willing to do this?'

"'Yes,' I replied with conviction. 'I can do that.'" Keanu paused, appearing to be reliving the past.

After a short pause, he spoke again.

"And that is what I did; I worked very hard! There were many times that my friends were playing games or watching movies and I really wanted to just hang out with them – but I remembered my goal – plus Eduardo kept encouraging me to stay true to my commitment. There were plenty of times that I felt like quitting – but I kept at it. It was well over a year, and then, in the Junior Championships, I ended up scoring a perfect score with five straight wins, to take first place and accomplish my dream in chess."

April clapped her hands, nearly bouncing out of her chair, she was so excited about Keanu's story – then paused as a thought struck her. "What happened after that? Did you set a new goal in chess? And how does this relate to your becoming a magician?"

Keanu smiled. "I quit studying chess the day after I achieved my dream of becoming junior champion. You see, I had a goal, and my commitment to that goal kept me going – and once my dream was accomplished, I just didn't want to study anymore. But what had happened was more profound, in that I had learned an invaluable lesson. I had learned that setting a goal is not enough!

That you must also carefully create your plan, and then commit to the effort needed to carry out your plan.

"It was just a short time after winning the junior championships that I had my introduction to magic. There was a small magic show put on by a local magician – and I was so captivated by what he did, that I bought a little magic kit from him that day, and that same night put on my first show!"

"Your first show that very day?" The surprise showed on April's face.

"Yes," Keanu smiled, "though the audience was a grand total of two – my parents. Still, I felt I had found my calling, my life calling. Immediately I just knew that I wanted to put on magic shows – I wanted to 'wow' and entertain others."

"What happened after that?" April asked, curious to hear the rest of Keanu's story.

"What I had learned from Eduardo I applied to magic," Keanu continued. "I set my sights on winning the national magic competition for my age bracket, and by applying the concept of planning, and then committing myself to the effort, that is indeed what happened. You could say that 'the rest is history.' From there it led to representing the U.S. in international competitions as far as Asia, developing my own show, and opening a theatre in the Bahamas, all before I turned 23."

Keanu's voice was earnest as he looked directly into April's eyes. "The reason I share all this with you, April, is that the person who was the catalyst in putting me on this path was Cathy. She's the one who took an interest in me, introduced me to the chess master, and encouraged me along the way. When she told me that there was someone she felt needed to hear my story, I knew that there was some very good reason she had for suggesting this meeting. I trust that my story will be helpful for you."

"Thank you," April replied softly. "I think I understand why Cathy wanted us to meet, and I'm very grateful to you and to

Cathy for taking the time and interest." As they both stood up April asked, "By the way, can I ask, just how did you do that with the giant chess piece? Was it really in the box or was that an illusion?" Keanu smiled. "I'm sorry, that I cannot share as that is a secret.

"But it's been a pleasure meeting you, April. And just remember, it's not what you see that matters – what matters is what you believe is possible. You saw and even held the Chess Knight. Even the seemingly impossible becomes possible if you dream it and believe it's possible. After that it's a matter of figuring out the steps needed in your plan, committing to the effort required, and letting the results take care of themselves."

The rest of the day, April had a hard time focusing on her school work because she kept thinking about what Keanu had said. As soon as school was released, she hurried down the hall, hoping to find Cathy. She had an idea she wanted to ask about. April was beginning to think that Cathy had already left for the day when she caught sight of her leaving the staff room.

April caught up with her, and blurted out, "Cathy, do you think he would help me make a plan?"

"Please slow down a moment, April!" Cathy replied. "Who do you mean? And which plan are you referring to?"

April continued. "I mean the chess master Eduardo – just like he helped Keanu develop a plan of exactly what to do and how much. Do you think he would help me with a plan for winning the championships? I really want to win the scholarship, and I'm afraid that without the plan I don't have much of a chance."

Cathy smiled, "I'm sure he would be happy to help you. I'll call him this afternoon and see if we can set up a meeting for later this week."

"Thank you so very much!" April smiled gratefully giving Cathy a quick hug. "I appreciate you and what you are doing for me."

"No need to mention it," Cathy replied with a smile. "It's a joy to help others. I believe that those who 'have' have a responsibility to use whatever they have received to help others. Sometimes that means giving monetarily, sometimes it means sharing knowledge, and sometimes it can be simply sharing one's life experiences with others."

Later that day as April reflected on what had happened; she found herself thinking more and more about the magician's box. "I wonder," she thought, "how many things are actually in my box and I've just thought it was empty. Well, I do believe I will discover what's in my box, but for now, I probably just need the plan. I can't wait to find out from Eduardo what exactly I need to do to win!"

That same week April indeed had the opportunity to meet up with Cathy and Eduardo. By the time they finished brainstorming, not only did April have a clear plan of what and how much to study each week, she also understood how to effectively put into practice what she was learning. She had a hard time containing the excitement she felt thanks to the clarity this gave her, and as she and Cathy returned from meeting with the master, she spoke confidently about her hopes of studying daily, for at least twelve hours a week, in order to gain the skill needed.

Cathy listened, smiled and nodded while thinking to herself how likely it was that April would need to meet another one of her friends. She anticipated that April was going to find her plan to be not quite as easy as she seemed to think at the moment. Cathy decided that now wasn't the time to bring up another deep topic, intuitively feeling that April needed to have time to let the current lesson on Planning settle in before adding the next key element.

CHAPTER 11

AS THE WEEKS passed by, April's commitment to her plan for achieving the big goal of winning the chess scholarship appeared to be paying off. Her confidence grew as she made steady progress in reading the essential chess strategy books Eduardo had recommended, and her results improved as she practiced chess every opportunity. It was becoming the norm for her to win more games than she lost. If someone asked April how many games she had won or lost, however, she would quickly reply that she had won all her games since she now eagerly sought to learn from every game she played regardless of the outcome.

One day after school, April had just left her classroom when Cathy came walking up. "April, could you plan on joining me after school tomorrow for about an hour?"

"Yes, that should work fine," April replied. "I was planning to study more chess, of course, prepping for the state qualifier tournament coming up in a couple weeks, but that can wait. What is it for?" April knew that Cathy must have something important in mind.

"Good," Cathy replied. "Please plan on meeting the team in Gabe's classroom. We can discuss it then. See you tomorrow!"

With that, Cathy turned to talk with another student, leaving

April wondering just what Cathy meant by the team that was going to meet her.

She decided it must have something to do with chess because it was in Gabe's classroom.

But...what team was this, and why did Cathy want her to meet with them?

The following day after school, April headed to Gabe's room. When she arrived, she found Gabe in his wheelchair with his pencil in his mouth as he worked away on what appeared to be math homework.

Gabe looked up as April entered, dropped the pencil onto the table, and smiled broadly as he welcomed her.

"Shake?"

April reached out and gave a quick shake to Gabe's foot, then sat down at the table ready to challenge Gabe to a chess game.

"Remember that first time we met? You looked as if you had somehow stepped onto another planet!" Gabe chuckled as he recalled their first meeting.

"Yeah," April replied with a smile, "you certainly surprised me!" As they played their opening moves, April spoke. "You know, Gabe, I don't think I've properly thanked you. You really have been such a big help to me. You've helped me gain the confidence to believe that I really CAN do this – that I can both play chess and achieve my dreams. I just want you to know how grateful I am." April was choking up with emotion, as thoughts came to mind of the months of intense effort to achieve her dream and all the progress she had made since that first-day meeting Gabe.

Gabe replied kindly, "It has been a pleasure to help in some small way, April. But seriously, I want to congratulate you on how far you've come. I feel as if I've had just a small part, perhaps simply being a catalyst that helped spark your discovery of your own abilities. You are the one who has put in the hard work so consistently. That is why the team has decided to invite you here today."

"What team?" April replied.

Just then Cathy entered the room, followed by three students April recognized from chess club.

As the students gathered around Gabe, Cathy smiled at April and then turned to Gabe. "Gabe, have you explained to April yet what this is about?"

Gabe replied, "Not yet. I was just about to when you arrived." Gabe looked at April and said, "April, the team Cathy mentioned to you is, as you're probably guessing already a chess team. Let me explain what makes this a unique team. We are a small group of students who are very diverse – many of us have had what others might call handicaps or unfortunate circumstances. However, what defines us as a team is our mindset: We all have a 'Can- Do Attitude' – we all see challenges as special opportunities – we believe that every person has a Unique Ability that simply needs opportunity to be discovered and developed."

Gabe paused and then continued, "April, as a team, we believe that you have demonstrated already the attitude and mindset of this team, and as such, we want to formally invite you onto the team. Are you willing to join us?"

April struggled to hold her emotions in check. She remembered how she had wanted so badly to make the sports team and failed – and now she was being invited to join this team!

"I would be honored to join your team," April replied softly. "I'm not sure that I have the full mindset of success that you mentioned, but I do try!"

Gabe smiled, "That's okay! All of us experience similar feelings. We are each on a journey of self-discovery – understanding our unique abilities, growing, making progress – and when things don't go well, we are there for each other, encouraging, supporting, and helping each other. You see, we believe that we are 'better together,' that we can go farther and accomplish far more together than we could alone."

As Gabe finished, the members of the chess team and Cathy clapped and welcomed April.

When the room quieted down, Cathy spoke, "Being able to support each other and work 'better together' improves the more that we understand and accept each other. April, whenever a new team member is invited and joins the team, we invite that person to share a bit about themselves. Would you be willing to share a bit of your story?"

"Sure, I would be happy to share with you," April said.

April started hesitantly at first, but as the team members listened, her confidence grew, and she shared about how she had overheard her parents talking about the financial challenges, how she so wanted to make the sports team in order to earn a scholarship, how she had been cut from the team, and how she had felt like a failure until Cathy introduced her to Gabe.

She paused, then took a deep breath and continued in a soft voice, "I've not shared this with anyone except Cathy, but I want you to know – I have a dream of winning the state championships chess scholarship in order to be able to help fund my college. Without it, I really don't see how we'll be able to afford the college I really want to attend."

When April had finished, the room was quiet for a few moments, then one of the students spoke up. "That is awesome, April! I'm sure I speak for us all in saying that we believe you can indeed accomplish your dream and that we will keep your dream in confidence among us until you decide to make it known. Thank you for sharing it with us."

The other students all nodded in agreement.

Cathy spoke up again. "Team, it seems to me that while you all work to achieve your goals, we all would like to help April fulfill her dream and win the scholarship. Am I correct?"

There was a resounding "Yes!" from all the students, and Cathy continued, "Each one of you on this team has experienced challenges, learned and grown. I'm really proud of how each of you is continuing to strive to become the best you can be, discovering and growing your own unique abilities. Chess is a game that I believe is truly a catalyst for discovering ourselves and developing what we could call "essential life skills" – skills that help a person navigate successfully through life. Many of these are 'mindsets' – meaning, as you know, how we think about things and how we respond to situations. To best help April achieve her dream, it seems to me that it would be helpful if April heard each of your stories that she hasn't heard yet, and what you learned through them."

The team nodded all around, and a student who with his blond hair and light blue eyes may have come from Scandinavian descent launched into his story first, smiling brightly as he spoke.

"My name is Oliver. I've been playing chess for several years, and I think I set the record in this school."

"Which record?" April interrupted.

Oliver laughed. "The record for the longest streak of losing games! It's not that I wanted to lose, but somehow, while I enjoyed playing, somehow my mindset was a failure mindset. No matter how good of a position I had, I always found a way to lose! I remember playing in a tournament one time, I had captured all my opponents' pieces except one rook, and I was about to promote one of my extra pawns into a new queen. That's when my opponent moved his rook checking my king – and my king was stuck behind my pawns on my own back rank – so there I was, checkmated again!

"Still, in spite of losing all these games, somehow I didn't lose interest. I think I enjoyed the challenges and the possibilities of the game. I sometimes wonder why the chess teacher didn't give up on me as a hopeless case," Oliver continued, looking at Cathy as he talked.

Cathy spoke up, "I remember the chess teacher talking to me about you after class one time. He said to me 'Cathy, I just don't know what to think about Oliver. I believe every person has some talent or another, but Oliver – his talent seems to be finding ways to lose every game he plays! No matter how many pieces of his opponents' he has captured, he always loses!' Oliver's teacher was surprised he hadn't given up on playing chess, and still seemed to enjoy coming to class, learning, and practicing. He wisely decided to keep encouraging Oliver to do his best and take his time – and just hoped for a breakthrough to occur before Oliver gave up."

Oliver nodded. "Yes, and that's exactly what happened. I think in looking back that I had somehow gotten into this mental state that I just couldn't win at chess, yet thankfully I kept trying. I remember playing tournament after tournament, losing every single game, until one day it finally happened. Once again, I had managed to lose my first four games. In the very last game of the tournament I was once again winning the game, but this time instead of finding a way to lose, I ended up getting a draw with my opponent by stalemating. So I didn't win, but I didn't lose either! I remember walking out of there so incredibly proud of not having lost – anybody seeing me walk out probably thought I had won the tournament!"

The other players were smiling and nodding, and Gabe spoke up. "And you remember, tell her what happened at the very next tournament."

"Yes," Oliver continued, "I won 3 games out of 5 and qualified for the state championships!"

"Wow!" April exclaimed. "How could you do that?"

Oliver replied, "You see, I believe I had the knowledge and even the skill by then. What I've come to understand though is that I simply had a mental block and a belief that I could only lose. Once that failure mindset was shattered by achieving the draw, suddenly I was free to utilize my abilities, and therefore the idea of qualifying for state – and scoring 3 out of 5 in the state championships as well – was no longer surprising to me."

"I think I understand," April said slowly. "You really had to develop the 'Can-Do' attitude. Not only that but what if you had given up along the way when it seemed as if you could never win a game! You could easily have quit, and no one would have been surprised. Instead, you persevered and kept at it."

"Yes," Oliver replied, "and I'm really glad I did. I don't have dreams of being chess champion, but I still very much enjoy the game and more importantly – in everything I do in school and life I have this experience that tells me no matter how many times I may fail along the way – don't give up!"

After Oliver finished his story, the team was quiet for a moment as they let the story sink in.

A tall, rather lanky student spoke up next.

"I'm glad you are joining the team, April. My name is Nikolai. I learned chess while still in elementary school. Unlike Oliver though, once I learned to play chess, I wanted to win – and badly! Losing was not an option. In fact, I couldn't handle losing well at all."

"You still don't like losing," Gabe broke in with a laugh. "You're right about that!" Nikolai replied, "But at least I handle it better than I used to!"

April felt there was an interesting story behind his reply. "Please tell me – I would love to hear your story," she said to Nikolai.

"Happy to!" Nikolai replied. "You see, in elementary school, I was in a class for autistic and other spectrum students. 'Retarded' was the word that other students often would say behind our backs – and to be mean, sometimes to our faces – though they learned not to say that in front of me as I would fight anybody I overheard say that."

Nikolai continued, "I think it was 2nd grade when I first discovered chess. There was a new afterschool chess club starting up, and my foster parents signed me up for the class as they thought it would be good for me. However, I think at the time they really just didn't know how to handle my emotional swings and were looking for ways to have me involved in any program that would allow me to join. I don't think the chess coach knew what was coming when I first joined. I learned the rules easily – it came to me naturally – but I couldn't stand to lose, and when someone would checkmate me, I would refuse to shake hands, sit sullenly, and often get so angry that I would throw the chess pieces on the floor or knock them all over and stomp off. If my opponent showed any sign of celebrating a win against me, I would get so angry that, more than once, I hit my opponents or threw a chess piece at them. I'm rather ashamed of how I behaved back then."

Nikolai paused, and then went on. "I'm really glad that the chess coach didn't give up on me! It would have been easy to simply say that I had broken the rules and to suspend me from chess class – but he didn't. Instead, he seemed to take a real interest in me and my challenges, and he kindly but firmly showed that he cared. He listened, talked with me, and at the same time let me know there are consequences for actions. He gave me a couple warnings, spoke with my foster parents, and finally one day after another one of my outbursts triggered by being checkmated, he sat down with me.

"'Nikolai,' he said gently, 'We've talked about this before, and you've had a couple warnings. What did we say would have to happen if you were to react like this again?'"

Nikolai continued, "I didn't say anything – I was angry and upset, and I didn't want to say what I knew – that he had said I would have to be suspended from class if I had another outburst. The coach continued in a kind but firm voice, 'Nikolai, as I told you before, now it has to happen – I'm suspending you from chess class. However, it is for just three weeks. I want you to use this time to think about how your actions have consequences, how you must learn to control your emotions and not let your emotions control you. If you are ready to do that, you will be welcomed back.'

"I was very upset," Nikolai said, "but I also knew the coach was a man of his word, and I was afraid that if I did anything else he might ban me from coming back forever.

"Those three weeks were some of the hardest I ever had. There were times I felt like never coming back because I was so upset – but I really liked playing chess! I felt I could do well; I really liked to win; and more, I felt that in chess class I was accepted and valued by the coach even though he could be firm. He was always fair and understanding. I didn't want to lose that. Plus, when I played chess, I got to play with all students – I was part of a group that wasn't defined by being special needs. I was awkward and uncoordinated – I really couldn't physically participate in sports – but in chess club, it was all about how you think, and I really felt I could win.

"After three weeks, I showed up to chess club again and sat down in the back. The coach saw me enter, and as soon as he could, he walked over to me and said quietly, 'Nikolai, welcome back. Are you ready to accept what I told you?'

"I nodded.

"Coach said, 'Then you need to go apologize to the student you were playing last time and ask his forgiveness for how you reacted.' I really didn't want to, but I knew Coach was right and I also really wanted to be in class, so I went over and apologized to him.

I guess in some ways you could say that was the start of a new friendship and the turning point for me!"

"Yeah, that was probably the hardest move you ever played against me!" chuckled Cho.

April looked at the fourth team member in surprise, "You were that other student?"

"Yes," Cho replied with a smile. "And I thought for a time that I was going to receive a black eye!" Cho laughed and winked at Nikolai.

Nikolai laughed also and continued. "What happened after

that was rather like a dream. Developing self-control over my emotions gave me opportunities I had never dreamed of. You see, I've learned now that students with some forms of autism can do very well in certain areas, yet frequently lack the EQ or emotional maturity necessary to flourish. If the EQ can be developed, they can excel in many areas.

"After that experience, in every class, I strived to keep my emotions in check, and with practice, it became easier. While even now it still requires effort, it's rare for me to get even close to losing my temper.

"With this emotional balancing, my grades started to improve. In fact, as my chess skills improved, my grades improved so dramatically, that my teachers were surprised and didn't know what to think! All they could say to my foster parents was 'we don't know what to say, but whatever you are doing, it's working – keep it up.'

"After a couple of years, I was moved out of the special needs classes into a regular classroom, and ultimately started earning straight A's.

"Along the way, my chess skill improved rapidly as I dedicated all my spare time to studying and practicing chess, and eventually had the opportunity to represent our state in an interstate competition."

Nikolai paused for a moment, then continued again. "Out of all the awards I've been able to achieve in chess tournaments, there is one that is my most treasured award, and it had nothing to do with my chess score."

"What was that?" April was leaning forward intently listening. "This award came two years after I had returned to chess class. During one of the semesters, I started helping other students who were struggling, and at the end of the semester, in front of all the students, our chess coach awarded me with the coveted Sportsmanship Award." Nikolai's voice had dropped to nearly a whisper and April thought she spotted a hint of a tear in his eye as he spoke.

He continued, "That award means the most to me because it represents to me not just how much I had changed and grown, but even more it was the result of that coach's enduring care and love for his students – including me, in spite of all the challenges that I had given him and the other students."

"Wow," April said, as she sat there taking in all she had just heard.

After a minute, April broke the silence. "Cho, what is your story? You've obviously been playing chess a long time now – what did you overcome? What lessons have you learned through chess?"

"I would be happy to share my story too, April. However, time is about up for me, as I need to leave if I'm going to make it to my meeting with your brother," Cho replied with a smile.

"With my brother? What would you be meeting him for?" April was surprised.

Cho replied, "I'm vice president of the robotics club, and we have some key projects we are working on in preparation for the end-of-year showcase. How about we meet up here after school tomorrow, and I'll fill you in then?"

"Sounds good," April replied. "In the meantime, would someone – perhaps Nikolai, would you be willing to help me with some of my chess openings? Gabe always gets me in trouble in just the first ten moves every time we play," she said half-jokingly, half seriously.

"Happy to!" Nikolai replied with a smile.

As Cho stood up to leave, April spoke up. "Team, thank you all for inviting me into your group. I am honored and grateful for both your invitation and you being so willing to help me. I promise to do my best to learn and represent the team's values. I'm so happy to join you!"

Late that afternoon, April was in her bedroom to work on homework, but was feeling distracted with thoughts of all she had experienced that afternoon. Reviewing the lessons that each student had learned through various difficult experiences; she suddenly remembered the life skills chart that Cathy had given her quite some time before. She quickly got up and looked inside her closet – sure enough, it was still there!

April took the chart over to her desk, sat down, and started filling in some of the blanks as she thought about the essential life skills she had been discovering.

Her list grew:

Can-Do Attitude

Goal Setting

Respect

Win. Draw. Learn

Planning

Sportsmanship

April thought a bit more about how Oliver and Nikolai had persevered, as well as how the team had formed as they helped each other, and she added two more:

Never Give Up

Better Together

As she lay in bed that night, April smiled to herself as she thought of how proud her parents would be when they would learn of how she was now on a team! She decided she would figure out a way to surprise them, perhaps at the state qualifier tournament that was coming up next month. It was the last chance to qualify for the state championships, but she wasn't feeling worried about the result. She was quite confident she would qualify – indeed so confident, that her focus was turned to what she needed to do to be ready to win the scholarship beyond at the state championships. With dreams of her parents smiling as she accepted the scholarship, April drifted off to sleep.

CHAPTER 12

THE NEXT DAY, right after school was dismissed, April went looking for Cho and met him in the hallway by the school lockers. She noticed he was wearing the school uniform and looked like he was ready to go for a run.

"Hi Cho," she said. "I didn't know you were into sports!"

As he closed the locker, he turned to April with a smile. "Yes, being on the soccer team has been a fun journey! Are you still free to chat for a bit?"

"Yes," April said, "how about we sit outside today – it's nice out."

"Sounds good," Cho replied.

As they were making their way outside to one of the school benches, the principal came walking by and said, "Cho, are you ready for your interview tomorrow?"

"Yes," Cho said. "3 p.m., correct?"

"Yes," the principal replied. "See you then!"

"What was that all about?" April asked Cho as soon as they sat down on the bench.

"Well," Cho said (a bit embarrassed it seemed), "I've been asked to do an interview for a local paper. They are wondering how it is that I'm able to play on the soccer team, serve as vice president of the robotics club, and hold a 4.0 GPA, planning to pursue computer science at Stanford next fall." He chuckled, "Funny thing is, I don't think they know I'm also part of our chess team!"

April was surprised, and to be honest, a little intimidated too, hearing of Cho's accomplishments.

"How is that possible? I'm amazed that you can do all that at the same time," she said.

"I'll just tell them that it's because I'm Asian," Cho joked.

He continued, "Seriously though, there is a story here. You see, if you had known me back a few years, you wouldn't have expected me to be the one being interviewed tomorrow at all. Unless that is if the interview was about 'what's it like to be a talented underachiever from Asia.'"

April was intrigued and leaned forward. "Please tell me what happened! Why were you an 'underachiever' and what caused that to change?"

Cho leaned back on the bench and started his story.

"Well, you see, it was like this. My parents came through very difficult times in China and barely made it to the U.S. To come here they had to work incredibly hard – sacrifice nearly everything they had – and give up most things for the dream of coming to the United States. They are highly educated and have a mindset that nothing less than perfection is acceptable. Achieving top grades is an absolute requirement – even scoring 99% on a math test is considered a failure.

"They came here to the United States, and you can just imagine, having sacrificed so much of their life in order to achieve the dream of coming to the U.S., they wanted to give everything they gained to my sister and me. They expected us to realize the opportunity and huge advantages that we had by being born here and see the potential of what could be if we were to apply ourselves the way they did back in China.

"However, just like many of the friends I know who are also second-generation Americans, having grown up here in the U.S., we often don't have that same perspective. As a young child, imagine what it feels like to be made to study for many hours, to take extra tutoring classes, and to learn and practice one or two musical instruments (whether you like to play or not). Your friends at school are having a good time playing and enjoying movies, sleepovers, games, and just hanging out; meanwhile, your schedule is nearly 100% full, from 6 a.m. to 10 p.m. seven days a week it seems.

"I, like many of my Asian friends growing up in similar circumstances, consciously or unconsciously rebelled against the pressure. For me, I just didn't have any motivation – I do think that I have some talents and abilities."

"You mean a LOT of talents!" April burst in.

"Well, okay. Though how much of an accomplishment is natural talent versus simply the result of time and effort put into tutors, extra studies, and so on?" Cho said.

"Hmm, I suppose that is part of it," April said slowly.

"That's okay," Cho said, smiling. He continued, "I felt I couldn't be perfect, so there was no way I was going to be able to please my parents. I felt I would never be 'good enough,' unable to meet their expectations. With that, I developed habits of simply doing the bare minimum to avoid getting into too much trouble – which meant still working quite hard, but I had the mindset of giving up rather easily. When playing piano became difficult, I simply told my parents that I was more interested in learning violin – and with enough pestering, they eventually gave in and let me switch musical instruments. There again I had early success and progressed rapidly, but when it became difficult, once again I switched, this time to the cello.

"This was how life was for some time, I always felt frustrated, until one day my parents enrolled me in a new afterschool class (the one where I met Nikolai). I think they enrolled me for two primary reasons; chess is often perceived as a game for smart kids plus their friends' kids were all taking chess, and they didn't want me to appear to be behind others. Well, I did take a liking to the game! But more importantly, the chess coach took a similar interest in me as he did with Nikolai. Indeed, I've come to learn that he took this same interest in the lives of all of his students. He really understood the power of someone who cared for and mentored us carefully. He recognized what was going on in our lives and would talk with us about life in the context of the chess lessons.

"He used to talk with us about how we are 'better together.' He would say, 'Just like on the chess board, it's important to use all of your pieces' unique ways of moving to work together to accomplish your plan. If you bring your pieces out one by one, you'll simply lose them one by one. The same applies to life, working with others is a way to be stronger and accomplish more. Those who strive to do everything alone are much less likely to succeed than those who learn to identify the unique abilities of each person and combine them to achieve great things.'"

Cho continued, "Coach was very patient as he worked with us day after day, weaving in examples from real-life experiences, whether from his own life or our lives, to illustrate principles. After tournaments, he would celebrate our progress. He was very good about turning every loss into a 'learn,' and continually encouraged us to think beyond the moment, to dream big, and then to put together plans to achieve those dreams. He was often heard saying, with a smile, 'If you have no plan, you'll be sure to achieve it!'

"One time our school had several students, including myself, who qualified for the state championships. We were excited to go, my parents were really proud of me for qualifying, and we went to the championships."

"How did you do there?" April asked eagerly. "Did you win the championships?"

"No," Cho replied. "Actually, I was overconfident and in my first game moved too quickly and was shocked to lose. I didn't really believe what had happened, thought it was a fluke, and went back for round two where again I lost rather rapidly. That was the moment where I woke up to reality. I had just lost two games in a row. I wanted to quit. In fact, I went to my parents and said 'I want to go home – I want to quit.' They were shocked, not really sure what to do – shocked both by my losing two games so quickly as well as by my wanting to give up – an attitude that was inconceivable to them – and so turned to the chess coach for help."

Cho paused as he appeared to be thinking over the story that he had just related. Then he continued. "The coach was very busy as there were many students there, but when he understood what had occurred, he left the rest of the students with an assistant and sat down outside the tournament hall where we had a little space to talk. I wanted to quit and go home, but he seemed to sense that this was a moment of truth for me.

"He said to me, 'Cho, I understand how you are feeling – I've had some pretty devastating losses myself in tournaments and have felt like quitting also. However, let's think about it for a minute. Now's not the time to review the moves you played and learn from them – that can be done sometime next week perhaps. Do you think it was really lack of knowledge that led to your opponents winning these games? Were you perhaps thinking that you would win easily?'

"I hung my head when he said that," Cho continued, "because I knew that I had been completely sure that I would just win easily."

"Then Coach continued, 'Cho, I think this is a very important moment in your life.'

"I looked up at him, puzzled, 'Why do you say that?'

"Coach said, 'You've not been doing your very best, you've just been doing what is needed to 'get by,' haven't you?'

"I was surprised that Coach had figured me out. 'But Coach,' I said. 'I've been studying my chess and practicing and working hard at it.'

"'Yes,' Coach replied, 'but that is because you are enjoying chess, isn't it? Are you doing your very best in your school, music, and other activities that your parents consider good for you to be involved in?'

"Coach was indeed right, so I just stayed silent.

"'You see, Cho,' Coach continued, 'If you can accept the painful lesson that 'getting by' is not the way to succeed, that it takes commitment and courage, it takes striving to do your best, and it takes work to develop healthy habits instead of allowing unhealthy habits to develop – then you have a real opportunity here.'

"'What do you mean?' I said.

"'It seems to me that you've allowed yourself to develop the unhealthy habit of simply finding the path of least resistance. Yes, if you enjoy something, for a while you pursue it diligently, and you do it well – you have capabilities that simply need development. Once it becomes more difficult, when your initial excitement in something new wears off, you then appear to look for the easy way out. Am I correct?' Coach asked.

"'Yes, I think so,' I replied slowly.

"'Well, Cho, do you like feeling like a failure? Do you want to continue on that path and feel this way, or are you willing to make a change?' Coach asked kindly.

"'Well, what can I do? I've already lost two games!' I replied, my current situation coming back into view.

"'Here's what you can do,' Coach replied. 'Instead of thinking about the outcome you want, such as winning, let's turn instead your focus to what you CAN control, your habits. Remember how we worked on taking your time each move to consider your opponents' plans? Remember what to do when you think you see a good move?'

"'Look for a better move,' I replied.

"'Exactly. You see, the things we learn in chess class are really intended to help us develop healthy habits. If you will apply those habits, focusing on what you can control, simply leaving the results to themselves, you will be able to apply all of your energy to figure out the best move in each position. Does that make sense to you?' Coach asked, looking at me intently to see if I really did understand.

"'Yes, I think so,' I replied.

"'So,' Coach continued, 'what I want you to do is to pretend that we are about to go into the first round of the state championships – that there are only three rounds – and the only thing that matters is for you to focus on finding the best move each turn. I really don't care about the results – win, draw, or learn. All that matters is that you focus on your healthy habit of searching for the best move. Can you do that?'

"'Yes, I can do that,' I said, a little more hopefully.

"'Good, then let's go in to start your game. I'm sure the games are already starting for this round,' Coach said, as he walked with me to the table where my opponent was waiting."

"What happened?" April asked eagerly.

Cho continued, "Well, I ended up winning all three remaining games, earning one of the trophies. However, my real win was that this experience had woken me up to the fact that I had been choosing to be a failure; that in seeking the easy way out, I had been developing unhealthy habits that ultimately would lead to a future I didn't want. As time went on, I understood better how that even if life was challenging and felt too busy or controlled, that this was simply a season of life, that my parents (like my chess coach) had my best interest in mind, and that it would be best if I simply did my very best all the time.

"A funny thing happened after that," Cho added. "Things that I didn't enjoy and wanted to get out of doing started becoming more interesting and enjoyable as I strove to simply do my very best in everything I did. In fact, I ended up getting a perfect score on the math SAT recently."

"Well, you certainly have achieved a lot now. Your parents must be very proud of you!" April said.

"Yes, I would say they are at least much happier than when I was trying to take the easy road! I'm also now grateful for their pushing me to strive for excellence, as doing so has led to some pretty amazing opportunities. What's interesting is that the more I've striven for excellence myself, the less my parents have pushed. Our relationship is a lot more enjoyable, almost like I'm talking with friends and peers rather than with my parents," Cho said quietly. He then added after a pause, "You know, I'm so VERY grateful for my chess coach too. He cared about me and was a great mentor."

"I've heard both you and Nikolai talk so highly about this chess coach. Who is he?" April asked.

Cho replied with surprise "You don't know? Why you've already met him!"

"I have?" April was puzzled.

"Yes," Cho continued. "He is the chess master who came to the tournament at our school!"

"Oh, wow, that makes sense now," April said as she remembered how uplifted and encouraged she had felt while talking with Eduardo. "He really was a wonderful encouragement to me too – he certainly helped me believe that I really could achieve.

"Thank you, Cho – I appreciate your sharing your story with me. This has given me a lot more to think about, though I do have some questions," April said as they both stood up.

"Happy to chat further when we have time," Cho replied. "You could ask Eduardo – I heard he's planning to be at the State Qualifier. Or if you can't wait till then, just ask Cathy. You know that she's the one who started the chess program here and asked Eduardo to be the advisor to the program."

"Good ideas!" April replied. "Thank you again for taking the time!"

"My pleasure!" Cho answered with a smile and a wave as he jogged off in the direction of the soccer field. "Glad to have you on the team!"

CHAPTER 13

THE DAYS AND weeks leading up to the state championships qualifier seemed rather like a blur to April. She focused harder than ever before in her life on her studies during class time. She found herself able to complete much of her homework during class, giving her the time to intensify her preparation for the tournament.

Her daily routine was fast becoming a natural habit. She was waking early, managing to put in at least 30 minutes even before breakfast on her chess practice. Lunchtime usually found her with one of her new chess teammates, eating while discussing chess openings and other strategies. As soon as the last class of the day was dismissed, April could be found either in the computer lab working online or facing off with another of the chess team members in a game to sharpen their skills. Evenings at home she went to her room directly after supper, closing her door so she could continue her chess studies uninterrupted – though Max would still slip in at various times, rarely bothering to knock. She didn't mind that too much though. If he asked, she would sometimes play a chess game with him. He had stopped saying "girls can't play chess," as April had not only managed to checkmate him, she had won every game she played with him. The roles were quite reversed now, as occasionally she even took time to give him some tips on his play.

Max didn't like to lose though, so more often than not, he would play with the robotic arm in April's room while she studied chess.

On days when the school chess club met, you could count on seeing April eagerly trying out the chess strategies she had discovered that week. Here also, April was becoming known as an opponent not to be underestimated. She surprised even some of the highest-ranked players in the club. Weekends were a mix of activities, including taking care of Max when her parents were busy (which seemed to be more often than not) and putting in as much time as she could on her chess studies. Occasionally April would get to the point where she needed to take a break from the intense chess effort, and in those times, she found herself tinkering with the robotic arm. She had not forgotten her idea of surprising Gabe with the robotic arm if she could just figure out a way for Gabe to work the controls.

The Friday before the state qualifier, the chess team had gathered in Gabe's classroom to get in some final practice matches. Cathy came in with an announcement. "Hi team! I'm sorry to interrupt you, but I've got some exciting news. My friend Eduardo, the chess master, said he would come about an hour early to the State Qualifier so he can meet with you to go over some key tips that can help before the tournament begins. Please do your best to arrive early to join in for this opportunity. I'm sure it will be very helpful!"

The players cheered, and then quickly got back to their training games.

The next morning was Saturday. Sara was getting an early start busily putting things away, as her family's schedule made it seem impossible to keep the house in order during the week. As she went through a pile of mail, she found the latest report cards. She opened the envelope with April's name on it, looked at it – and then looked at the name on the card again. While April's grades were usually decent, they had never been exceptional – but this time they were the highest she had ever seen them! Report card in hand, she went to find her husband, who was slowly waking up after another late Friday night dinner with his co-workers.

"Davis, what do you make of this?" She handed the report card to him.

"Make of what?" He replied, smothering a yawn, as he stretched and took the report card. He looked at the card, read it – and then did just what Sara had done, looking at the name on the card again thinking that perhaps there was a mistake.

"Wow, I did not expect to see scores that high from April!" he said.

"Exactly!" Sara replied. "I don't know what to make of it. I know she 's been busier than usual for a while. She's been staying at school longer and going to her room earlier when home, but I assumed she was spending time with friends. I rarely see her doing any homework also, though she does seem to have taken a liking to playing chess lately. I am rather puzzled! Maybe it's just a fluke, and the latest tests were simpler for some reason."

"Let's just see how things continue, and we can always ask her teachers or student counselor next chance we have," Davis replied, sitting up.

"Sounds good," Sara replied as she went back to cleaning things up and starting breakfast.

As the family gathered around the breakfast table, April spoke up, "Dad and Mom, could someone drive me to school next Saturday at 8 a.m.?"

"What's going on at school?" Davis asked.

"There's a chess tournament I would like to play in. Several friends are going to be there," April replied.

"Not just any chess tournament!" Michael broke in with a smile. "I heard from my friend Cho that it's the Last Chance Qualifier for the state championships! And he says that the way you've been improving, you have a real chance of making it."

"Really? I had no idea you were that interested in chess," Sara said.

April really wanted to share her dream! That it wasn't so much about enjoying chess (though she did find it interesting), as it was her deepest wish to find a path to university – and that chess seemed like the path she could take to accomplish it. She couldn't yet put into words that she just wanted her parents to not have to worry about her future and she wanted them to be proud of her and what she could accomplish. Not able to share all this, she simply replied, "Yes, I would like to play in the tournament. And there's going to be a coach there to talk with us about how to do our best, which is why I need to be there so early."

"We'll make it work!" her dad said. "In fact, I would like to see you play if that's okay."

"I want to go too!" Max spoke up.

"Why don't we all go and support April?" Sara said. "Good idea!" Michael added.

In a short time, after comparing schedules, they figured out that Davis could drop April off before taking care of some client meetings and they could all gather at the tournament later to watch April compete.

The night before the tournament, April had trouble falling asleep, feeling already a little bit nervous as well as excited. She woke early the next morning and dressed quickly. She ate her breakfast in the car as they drove to the college gym where the tournament was being held.

"Good luck and see you soon!" Her dad smiled as she got out of the car. "Have fun!"

"Thanks, Dad!" she smiled back. She was secretly glad that her family was coming – while also rather glad they were not going to be there until later, as she was feeling more nervous than she had anticipated. "See you later!"

Cathy met April at the entrance. "Good morning, April! So glad you could make it this early!" she said with a bright smile.

Before long, the team had assembled, Gabe being the last one to arrive. Together the team helped him out of the special van for disabled students that brought him, and then they all followed Cathy to a classroom where the chess master was already waiting.

"Come on in!" he said with a smile. "Why don't you all take a drink of water or juice, then see how fast you can solve the chess puzzles I've set up." April noticed that there were six chessboards set up around the room, with various positions on them, as well as some juice cartons and a tray of sliced apples on a side table.

The team eagerly started solving the chess puzzles, moving from one board to another, solving them together. The puzzles started simply and moved to more complex positions, but together the team was able to figure them all out.

"Good work!" Eduardo commented as soon as they completed the last puzzle. "Now please pair up and work on these warm-up chess challenges." He pointed to the whiteboard where he had written out a variety of chess positions for them to practice, starting with several checkmate practice drills. "Once one partner accomplishes the checkmate, do the same activity again, just switching sides so that you each get the opportunity to do the checkmate."

The team members worked through the challenges quickly, with Eduardo occasionally giving a tip or suggestion.

April found her nervousness disappearing and her confidence rising as she completed the challenges.

Once they had all completed the challenges, the master said: "Okay, please reset all the boards, then move your chairs to form a small circle here with me."

The team worked quickly together and gathered in a circle. Once all were seated, Eduardo spoke quietly. "How do you feel?"

"I'm excited for the tournament! A little bit nervous still though," April replied. Others nodded their heads in agreement.

"This is a big tournament – I think there are over 300 players! I hope we all make it to State," Nikolai said.

Eduardo considered this. "Yes, I understand that is your goal today – you all want to ensure that you qualify for the state championships! Now, in order to be most ready, there are a few things that I have found to be most helpful for performing my best in competitions. Would you like to hear them?"

"Yes!" the team replied nearly in unison.

"Well, let me start by telling you a story from one of the large national chess tournaments I've attended. I was a master level player by this time and attended the event as I was coaching several promising students there – one of whom would later go on to become the number one player in the United States for his age. Because this competition was open to all ages, in addition to coaching I also was competing.

"One of the rounds, I found myself paired against a girl who was rated over 2000 though still more than 200 rating points below my rating. When I came to the board, I was surprised to find out that she must have been only about 12 years old – so obviously an up-and-coming player.

"As the game began, I played carefully, developing all my pieces, controlling the middle of the board, and slowly advancing to gain more space. I was able to build a small advantage, and while my opponent defended very well, I was able to build upon the advantage until there was tremendous pressure on my opponent's defenses."

The team leaned forward, listening intently as Eduardo's telling of the story made them feel as if they were living the experience.

"Eventually after over two hours of intense concentration and battling it out over the board, I found a way to win one of my opponent's pawns. As my opponent studied the position realizing that she was going to lose a pawn, I mentally relaxed thinking that it would now simply be a matter of time before I would be able to use my extra pawn to advance across the board, promote it into another piece, and then go about finishing the game. Waiting for my opponent to decide on a move, I started wondering how my students were doing and decided to check on them.

"I walked around the tournament hall taking a quick look at each of my students' games in progress, stopping to look at one in particular, that was a very close game with both sides having chances. After looking at that position for a minute, I returned to my own game.

"My opponent made her move just as I returned. I sat down, looked briefly at her move – and then made my move. The moment I made a move, I suddenly saw that I had just made a big mistake, missing another move she could play that would likely win one of my pawns!

"Sure enough, she saw the best move and played it.

"I was immediately frustrated with myself for my big mistake that gave up all the advantage it had taken over two hours to gain and after thinking for just a little bit, I made another move figuring that now I would either have to settle for a draw or work really hard to try to find another way to win.

"My opponent looked at my move in surprise and made her move instantly. I couldn't believe it – but as I stared at the board, I came to the realization that I had made another big blunder and this time I was going to either lose a whole rook or get checkmated! I lost the game just a few moves later."

April and the rest of the chess team let out a chorus of 'Oh no,' and April realized that she had been holding her breath, listening so intently to the story Eduardo was telling.

"You must have felt terrible!" Cho said, and the rest of the team nodded their heads.

"Yes, you're right, I did feel terrible. Perhaps you are wondering why I would share this story right before you begin your tournament?" Without waiting for an answer, Eduardo continued.

"As I was reviewing later on what led to my losing that game, I realized there were several very valuable lessons.

"First, I started off very well. Even though I knew my opponent was rated considerably lower than myself, I had managed to avoid being overconfident and simply focused very carefully on finding the best moves in the position, building up to the point where I won a pawn.

"Second, while my focus had been excellent to that point and I had not gotten up once during that whole time, winning the pawn combined with thinking that my opponent was much less experienced led me to become overconfident, thinking that it would just be a matter of time before I would win the game.

"Third – and probably the most important lesson from this game – I left the board to look at another game, breaking the focus that I had maintained till that moment. Losing that focus led to my missing the other move that my opponent had found, leading to the next lesson.

"Fourth and last, I moved too quickly after realizing my first mistake while still trying to emotionally recover from the realization that I would likely not win and might have to settle for a draw. This led to the big blunder that cost me the game."

When Eduardo finished, he let the team reflect for a minute on what he had just shared, then continued.

"Team, the reason I share this story with you, is that over time I have become very thankful for that painful experience. I learned so much from that game and have been able to share these lessons with many students. And today, I wanted you to learn from my experience so that you can be ready for today's event. Can you summarize for me what your takeaways are, that you can apply today?" Nikolai spoke up, "It seems to me that we will do well if we go into every game with the Can-Do Attitude, in addition to showing Respect for all our opponents by not being overconfident."

"Focus on my game only without looking at other games in progress, staying at my own board, will help me do well whether I Win, Draw, or Learn," Gabe said.

April added, "Also if we realize during the game that we've made a mistake or missed something, we should slow down to regain our focus instead of moving too quickly."

"Well said," Eduardo replied. "Now think about that game of mine from my opponent's perspective. My young opponent was playing against an older, much more experienced and master-level player. Was she intimidated? No! She went into the game with focus, doing her best with a Can-Do Attitude and worked very hard to defend the position, never giving up! Even when she realized she was going to lose a pawn, which could very well signal the end of the game coming soon, she did not give up but kept on looking for any opportunities. As a result, she found some other ways to defend.

"With that, thanks to my losing focus and blundering, she not only won the pawn back – she won more material and then the game."

Eduardo paused, looked at every one of the team and then said slowly and intently, "Team, today you will be competing with others of varying skill levels. If you apply the lessons from my experience, regardless of who is sitting across from you, you will be able to do well. Does that make sense to you?"

As the team nodded, Eduardo stood up.

"Very good! Now let's cover the other key elements to be best prepared. It boils down to a series of 'Healthy Habits' and mindsets. You've done your preparation already in terms of chess knowledge. Now you must trust that knowledge and practice, and simply strive to 'get into the zone' – the mental state where you have blocked out other inputs, and your mind is focused solely on solving the chess puzzles you face every move of the game."

Eduardo walked the team through a short series of tips, then wrapped up the session with one final exercise where he had the team all close their eyes, take several slow and deep breaths, and imagine themselves playing their first moves in the tournament.

"Ok, it's time to go!" Eduardo spoke with enthusiasm. "Please be sure to write down all the moves you play so we can learn from them later, stay focused on just your own game, and have fun!"

He high-fived the students as they left the classroom to head into their first match.

The team returned one by one to the classroom as they each finished their game, and when the last person had come in, they let out a loud cheer. Everyone on the team had won their first game!

Her first win exhilarated April, but the second round she played a long hard game that ended up with her opponent promoting a pawn and checkmating her. The day progressed until she found herself with just the last game to play and still needing one more win to qualify for the state championships.

The rest of the team had already qualified for State, but April was feeling rather uncertain. She tried to focus on the tips the chess master had given, but it was hard to keep thoughts of failure from creeping in.

Cathy noticed how quiet she was, came over to her, and said quietly, "Remember what Cho shared with you – how he once lost his first two games and wanted to quit?"

April nodded.

"Remember what helped him come back to win the last three games?" Cathy continued.

"Healthy habits," April replied. "Focusing on just one move at a time, not worrying about the results."

"Yes." Cathy added, "Why don't you just keep that in mind? And just like Cho did once, pretend that this next game is the first game of the tournament. Simply try to focus on what you know already. You do indeed have the ability as well as the skill you need! I KNOW you can do it!"

April smiled a little, "The 'Can-Do Attitude' again. Yes, you are right. I'll do my best, and I do believe I can. I'll just do my best to focus on one move at a time."

As April walked towards the tournament hall for her last game, she heard her dad's voice suddenly, "April!"

April turned and saw her dad coming down the hall, with Sara right behind. "Sorry it took us so long," Davis said. "We got here as soon as we could. We're all here excited to support you!"

"Thank you for coming!" April said and gave her parents a quick hug.

"You can do it!" Michael called after her, as she left them to find her seat in the crowded tournament room.

The room was quiet as the games began, the only sound the clicking of chess pieces on the board. The suspense of the final round seemed to fill the room. Players who had finished, along with family members, gathered together in the 'skittles room.'

April and her opponent battled hard, and they entered a tense endgame with just a few pieces left on the board. April didn't notice when her game was one of the last games still in progress in the tournament. She was intently focused on calculating whether she could promote a pawn before her opponent – it was going to be very close. She thought very carefully, and then started to get excited as she thought she saw a way to win! She paused though, internally fighting the excitement, and telling herself, Focus, April! Stay focused! Just look for the best moves – forget about the result! She looked even more closely and saw that they would both end up promoting. That's no good, she thought – I need to find a way to promote first!

Then she saw it…

April quietly pushed her pawn forward. Her opponent

responded by pushing his pawn as well, and they made the series of moves she had anticipated. Then, right before promoting her pawn, April inserted another move first, checking her opponent's king and forcing the king to move where she wanted it. Next move, she would be able to promote her pawn – not only promoting but doing so with check, and thus being able to prevent her opponent from also promoting!

April's opponent paused with a look of shock on his face. He looked at the board as the realization that he had missed April's surprise move sunk in. After a minute he looked at April and reached out to shake hands, "I resign – you win. Good move! You really did that well!"

"Thank you for the game!" April replied as she shook hands with him.

April quietly reset the chess pieces and walked – or rather floated – out of the room, hardly believing that it was real!

Her family and team were waiting outside the playing hall. As she came through the doors, her face must have shown the result, as they all burst out cheering.

April ran to her dad and gave him a hug. "I'm so glad you came!" she said.

"I'm so proud of you!" Sara said. "You really surprised me. You did very well!"

The team, as well as her family, gathered around congratulating her, and April beamed as she told them of finding the move that allowed her to win.

April suddenly realized that Gabe was missing from the group. "Where's Gabe?" she said.

Someone replied, "Last I saw he was still battling it out on the top board!"

Just then Gabe came rolling in on his wheelchair. "How did you do, April?" he called out almost before he was in the room.

"I won!" April replied and ran to meet him.

Gabe let out a loud cheer, "Hurray, April! I knew you could do it! You've qualified for the state championships!!"

"Thank you, Gabe," April said. "How did you do? What happened in your game?"

Gabe replied slowly as he shook his head, "It was close. I thought I had him, and I did – but then I got too low on time. I took a bit too long on some moves, then made a blunder."

Gabe was quiet, and April sensed his disappointment – and guessed at what had happened. With his physical limitations, getting low on time in a game meant that he had to rush his moves, as it just took him too much time to navigate moving the pieces on the board. Moving quickly sometimes led to making blunders. Gabe quickly brightened again, though. "Good news is – my opponent was one of the best, and now he just might be overconfident when we meet at State! I'll get my rematch there. And just think – we've ALL qualified for State – the whole team! I think it's time for a celebration!"

The rest joined in with another cheer and high-fived all around.

In the midst of their celebrating together, however, April kept thinking about Gabe's loss.

There's got to be a way that the robotic arm could have helped him win that game, she thought to herself. *I'm going to find a way.*

CHAPTER 14

"**W**HY DON'T YOU ask Michael?"

Max's question caught April by surprise. She was in her room where she had planned to work on her prep for the state championships, but the memory of Gabe's loss at the state qualifier that had prevented him from winning the tournament kept interrupting her studies. She had pulled out the robotic arm and was absent-mindedly dreaming of how it could be used to help Gabe when Max's question brought her back to the present.

"What do you mean?" April asked.

"Well, you want to help Gabe, don't you? Michael's president of the Robotics club – seems to me they could be of some help, don't you think?" Max replied matter-of-factly.

April was surprised by Max's intuition. "How did you know that I was thinking about how to use this robotic arm to help Gabe?" she asked.

"You looked like you were going to cry on Saturday when you heard Gabe lost, and your face looked the same now – so I just guessed," Max said. "Are you going to ask Michael?"

"Thanks for the reminder! I will," she said. "In fact, he should be home any time now, I think."

April couldn't wait to ask Michael. She was sure he would be able to give her some advice.

When Michael came home shortly after, he was barely in the door when April ran up to him. "Michael, can you help me, please? Can you help with the robotic arm I want to give to Gabe?"

"Whoa, not so fast! What robotic arm? What's this all about?" Michael replied in bewilderment.

"Come, let me show you!" April replied. "It's in my room."

Michael put his backpack down and followed April to her room. "Why don't you slow down just a bit and fill me in on what you have in mind. I'll be happy to help once I know what this is all about!"

April showed Michael the Robotic Arm that she had assembled from the kit. She demonstrated it, picking up a few items. Then she filled Michael in on her story of how she had learned chess from Gabe, how she had seen his challenges with picking things up, and how at the tournament on Saturday it had become painfully clear to her that he had lost his chance to win the whole tournament because of his physical handicap – and how much she was hoping to make the robotic arm into a tool that would help him.

Michael listened quietly as she spoke, and when she finished, he replied slowly. "April, I'm really happy to hear of this awesome idea! You've already made a ton of progress I can see. I think you're really close. You're already using this robotic arm nearly like a replacement hand. What do you think is the biggest challenge to making it work for Gabe?"

"Well, you see," April said, "Gabe has one foot that functions rather like a hand on a short arm. He's able to use his toes better than many folks can use fingers. However, that's his only 'hand'! If we strap this robotic arm onto it, then while he may be able to use this robotic arm, it will likely block him from using his foot for other things. While it may be helpful in some situations, it may get in the way the rest of the time."

"I see you've thought about this carefully," Michael replied. "Hmm, I wonder... Okay, what if you could strap the robotic arm onto Gabe's upper body where his arm should be, and then use a remote control that his foot could operate?"

"That's a great idea!" April exclaimed. "That would be awesome if it works. Maybe if we had a touchscreen control of some kind? If we could mount it on his chair near his foot, then he could control it that way. And then the robotic arm would be not just an extension but an additional arm! Oh, that's exciting! I'm sure that will work!"

Together they talked it through, figuring out what else they thought would be needed. First, they needed to acquire a touch screen controller, and see if they could program it to match the controls on the robotic arm. Then they needed to figure out an adapter to tap into Gabe's motorized wheelchair, rather than rely solely on battery power in the robotic arm. Finally satisfied that they had figured out a solution, and eager to put the plan into action, Michael said, "I should be able to figure out the power options. In fact, I'll plan on seeing what I can do on that tomorrow. But for the touchscreen, you may want to ask Dad. My guess is through his work he should at least know where a touchscreen controller like we are thinking of could be found."

"I'll ask him tonight," April replied. "Thanks very much for helping me."

"Happy to!" Michael replied with a smile.

April hoped her dad wouldn't be delayed at work again. She kept looking for her Dad's car, but it wasn't until after supper had been cleared away and it was getting close to her bedtime that she heard him pull into the driveway.

She barely waited for Davis to get in the door when she met him and asked, "Dad, can you please help me with something?"

Davis smiled, a little surprised by her enthusiasm and not used to receiving requests from April. "As long as you're not asking me to solve a chess puzzle, I'll be happy to help!" he teased.

April led him to her room, where she showed him the Robotic Arm and then told the story of how she had come up with her idea, what she had already done, and what she was hoping to accomplish with it to help Gabe.

Davis listened quietly, and when she finished, he said, "You know, April, you keep surprising me. Qualifying for the state chess championships – now this Robotic Arm. That's quite amazing! Even more, I love how you are trying to use this to help Gabe. I was quite impressed with Gabe's attitude and abilities in spite of his disabilities when I met him at the tournament. For sure, I will be happy to help. I do think we have at work what you need. There are some new game controllers just in, and I'll check tomorrow if I can get permission to have one – shouldn't be a problem."

April clapped her hands together quietly, "Thanks, Dad! I appreciate that!" She gave him a quick kiss on his cheek.

"You're welcome! Happy to help," he said. "Good night!"

⌇

The next evening Davis arrived home just as the rest of the family was finishing dinner.

"Dad, did you get it?" April asked eagerly, jumping up and running over to him as he came in.

"Sure did!" He answered with a smile, waving a small bag. "Oh, thank you, Dad! That's great!" April beamed. "Can we start on it right away?"

"Why don't you all go right ahead – I'll clear the dishes and fix up a plate for you at the same time so you can get started right away," Sara said, happy to see them working together on a project. Davis handed April the bag he had brought home. "Here, would you like to open this and see if we can make that work? And Michael, I was able to pick up a few different converters just in case we need one. How about we tackle the power supply?"

"Sounds good," Michael answered, pulling out a few cables as well as a couple of tools from his backpack.

April didn't answer as she was already engrossed in opening

the bag. Inside she found a new touchscreen game controller. April plugged the touchscreen controller into the software program that came with the Robotic Arm and was pleased to find that it was compatible. She was able to program the buttons needed to match up to the controllers on the Robotic Arm, and while she did that, Michael and Davis were working on the power supply options. Within a short time, they were ready!

They took turns testing the remote-controlled Robotic Arm and found that it worked quite well. April made a few adjustments to the settings so that it would move more smoothly.

"When are you going to give it to Gabe?" Davis asked April when they had finished.

"Well, tomorrow is Wednesday, and we have a chess team meeting in Gabe's classroom. I think at the start of the meeting would be a good time. I'll see if Cathy can bring it to the room as a surprise after we are all in there."

"If you like, I can bring it to Cathy early – I'll be seeing her before school tomorrow. That way there's no chance of Gabe seeing you with it before the afternoon," Michael volunteered. "Plus, I would love to come and see Gabe when he tries it out. That is if you don't mind."

"Yes, thank you! That sounds like a good plan," April replied. The next day April had a hard time focusing on her school-work as she kept thinking about how surprised Gabe would be. As soon as the last bell sounded, she rushed off towards Gabe's room. "What's the hurry? Is there a fire?" Teegan's voice interrupted April.

"I've got an important meeting," April replied as she continued down the hall.

Teegan stepped in stride beside April, "Are you trying to make him your new boyfriend?"

April stopped nearly mid-stride and looked at Teegan. "What do you mean? Who are you talking about?"

"Cho, of course!" Teegan replied. "It's obvious. You've started playing chess, going to a tournament, hanging out with the group that meets away from the others in Gabe's room – and who's the only good-looking guy in the group?"

April thought about replying sharply, but she had come to think that Teegan's comments were likely masking insecurity, and decided to just brush off the comments.

"If you want to come in about 20 minutes to the chess team meeting, you can find out for yourself!" April answered with a smile. "You just might be more confused – or not, and hey, maybe you can learn chess and join us!"

"I'm rather busy, or I just might take you up on that," Teegan answered, apparently not quite sure what to make of April's confident reply.

"Up to you!" April called over her shoulder as she moved on towards Gabe's room.

When she arrived, she found the rest of the team already there, working on solving a few chess puzzles that one of the team had found recently.

"Hi, April! Ready to win the championships?" Gabe called out as April entered the room. "Congrats again on qualifying – and I'll bet you win the champs."

"Well, thanks to your help and so many others, I think I've got a chance at least. I'll do my very best for sure," April replied.

April noticed Cathy entering the room, followed closely by Michael, who carried a plain box. April was glad they had figured a way to make the surprise plan work out. No one but her would know what was in that box!

Cathy came over to April and whispered in her ear, "Michael filled me in on what you've been doing – I'm really proud of you! Whenever you're ready, go ahead."

April nodded and replied simply "thank you," though the words of praise from Cathy meant more to her than she let on.

It was time! April stood up and spoke, "Chess team, may I have your attention for a minute! I've got something I want to share."

The players took a break from their practice and looked up. Suddenly, even though it was a small group that she had gotten to know quite well over the last few months, she found herself feeling a bit nervous standing in front of them all.

"Well," she started hesitantly, "I just wanted to say a few things. I've been so grateful to Gabe for teaching me how to play chess, and the many times he's continued to encourage me while patiently helping me develop chess strategies." April was growing bolder as she spoke. "He's also given me confidence that I can indeed achieve. That no matter our circumstances, we should focus on what we have instead of what we do not have, and by discovering and developing our own unique abilities, we can indeed make progress towards accomplishing our dreams. I've admired how Gabe always focuses on the positive, even when he lost the last round of the state qualifier."

April saw by the faces of her team members, as well as the heads nodding that they all agreed with her.

She continued. "I've had an idea for quite some time of something that may help Gabe – and I think it's ready now!" April went to Michael, took the box from him, and set it on the table in front of Gabe.

"Gabe, you've been truly an inspiration to me, and I think also to many others. This is a gift for you that I hope can be of help to you in return." As she spoke, April opened the box and lifted out the robotic arm. "This is a robotic arm. I thought that it could help you by giving you an extended reach. In chess tournaments, this could perhaps help you reach the chess pieces and timer more easily, so you don't lose because of time. What do you think? Would you like to try it on?"

Gabe nodded, apparently for once unable to speak. With Michael and Cathy's help, April put the robotic arm in place, adjusting the straps around Gabe's shoulders to hold it firmly.

April then reached back into the box and pulled out the

touchscreen controller. She explained it as she mounted the controller near Gabe's foot. "You see, this controller here is a remote controller for the Robotic Arm. You turn it on by pressing this button on the side – then the screen has the controls to do the rest."

April explained how to work the Robotic Arm to Gabe, then stepped back. "Ok, why don't you try it?"

Gabe carefully touched the buttons, and the Robotic Arm responded, moving forward. He maneuvered it carefully forward, reaching out and picking up a chess queen from beside the board, moving it onto the opposite side of the chessboard. When he released the piece onto the square, he found his voice again. "This is AMAZING! I don't know what to say. Thank you, April! Thank you!" There were tears in his eyes, and his voice choked. "I don't know that anyone has done something so amazing for me. The thing that comes closest is the man who sponsored my coming to America for school."

April gave him a hug and said, "You're very welcome, Gabe! Though to be fair, it wasn't just me – sure it was my idea, but I had help. My brother Michael figured out the power supply adapter; my dad provided the touchscreen game controller as well as the original Robotic Arm – even Max helped out. In many ways, it's just like I've learned in chess. The chess pieces work 'Better Together,' and you rarely succeed if you play with just one at a time. So here, with all of their help, we've been able to put this together. I hope it helps you out in many ways."

"I just might need to steal you away from the chess team to join the Robotics Team instead," Michael said jokingly with a smile.

The rest of the team gathered around Gabe as he played with the Robotic Arm, examining it carefully.

"Wow, that's amazing – you actually did that?" Teegan's voice at April's side nearly made her jump. She hadn't noticed that Teegan was listening in at the doorway, while she had presented the Robotic Arm to Gabe. There was a newfound respect and even a sense of awe in Teegan's voice.

"Yes, though I had a lot of help," April replied.

"I wish I could do something like that," Teegan replied quietly. "I'm not good at anything."

"Oh, I'm sure you can. You just need to discover your own unique ability, and then work to develop it," April replied, surprised by Teegan opening up so much about what was really going on inside of her, and wanting to encourage her in some way. "If you like, we can talk about it sometime."

"I'd like that," Teegan replied. "Thank you."

Cathy stood off to one side watching as the chess team settled into their training for the afternoon; Gabe was focused more on using his Robotic Arm than on finding the best moves. She smiled to herself. April was continuing to surprise her, blossoming in more ways than even she had imagined. She had high hopes for the upcoming chess championships – she felt that the team was going to score well and possibly even win a team award. Even though it was still a big stretch, she felt that April too really did have a chance at winning the scholarship she had been dreaming about for so long. Cathy decided it was time to ask her friend Eduardo the chess master for help with one more key lesson that she felt the team – and April – really needed to be fully ready.

As was her habit, once she made up her mind about something, Cathy didn't waste any time. She headed out of the chess team meeting to give Eduardo a call immediately. As she had expected, he was more than happy to take the time to come out and meet with the team later that week.

CHAPTER 15

THE CHESS TEAM gathered in Gabe's room once again, expectantly waiting for the chess master Eduardo to arrive.

Cathy had let the team know that he was coming to help them prepare for the state championships, and they were eager to hear what he would share with them.

When he arrived, he started right in.

"Hi everyone! Let's get started right away. We don't have much time, and these state championships are coming up quickly," Eduardo said, even as he walked towards the front of the room where there hung a whiteboard.

"Okay, let's begin with a review of the essential skills for success that you have covered already. Who would like to name one first?" he asked, looking around the room.

"Do you mean like the habit of always looking for a better move and taking your time?" Cho asked.

"Yes," Eduardo replied as he wrote it on the whiteboard. "That would fall under what we call Healthy Habits as it includes multiple habits that help you perform better. What's another?"

"Can-Do Attitude!" April called out.

"Very good!" Eduardo replied, writing that down next.

The team worked together calling out various ones until they had quite a list.

Healthy Habits
Can-Do Attitude
Win.Draw.Learn.
Goal Setting
Planning
Better Together
Sportsmanship
Respect

"How about Focus?" Nikolai asked.

"Good idea," Eduardo replied, "though I find that in many cases Focus is something that is often the result of the other skills such as 'Healthy Habits.' Do you see how that can be?"

"You mean because that as we take our time and look for better moves – and perhaps as we respect our opponents no matter their skill level – we will look at only our own games, focusing on finding the best moves – and that develops our Focus?" Cho answered. "Well said!" Eduardo replied. "That is exactly what happens.

I've seen it occur over and over again with hundreds of students."

He continued, "Now that you all have qualified for the state championships, there is one more essential skill that I would like to share with you. I find it's simplest to understand if I just share another story to illustrate it. Would you like to hear about it?"

"Yes!" the team said, all heads nodding.

"This story is again from my own experience," Eduardo said, "when I was about your ages, and based on rating was becoming one of the favorites to win the state high school championships. I was competing two or even three times per month, studying hard, and working my best as I really wanted to win the championships. However, there were a few other players who I knew were also keen on winning the championships and were doing their best to defeat me also.

"Well, at one of these events I played one of these opponents in a very tough battle on the board, and I was able to squeeze out a win eventually. The next week, as I was continuing my studies, I thought to myself, 'That was a really close game. What if I have to play this same opponent next event also? What can I do to be better prepared for next time?' With that thought, I took a look at the record of the game we had played. Note that I always wrote down every move in every tournament I played," Eduardo smiled. "In looking through the game carefully, I found the move where the game had really turned in my favor thanks to my opponent overlooking a move, and I thought to myself, 'I'll bet he's also going to find this spot and he's going to try to find a better move in this position. What will I do if he does so?'"

The team listened intently as Eduardo continued the story. "Well, after looking carefully, I found a different move for my opponent that would have ended up with at least a draw – I didn't see any way I could win if my opponent had played this improvement. And I certainly wasn't interested in just getting a draw next time! I started searching earlier – and just a few moves prior to the key position, I found a move that I could have played which would have given me a good position, and was quite dangerous for my opponent. After considering the possibilities for a while, I decided that if I happened to get to the same position with this opponent again, I would at least be ready for him. And guess what? That's exactly what happened!

"We were matched up with each other at the very next tournament. I was once again playing the dark pieces, and we repeated the moves from our first encounter. My opponent played rather quickly, which led me to believe that he indeed must have figured out an improvement, so when we got to the key position where I had planned to deviate, I made my move and waited to see his reaction. He thought for a very long time before making his move, and from there on he played quite slowly. I was able to gain a small advantage, and he defended well, but I was able to pull out the win again."

The team clapped their hands as they listened to this story, but

Eduardo held up his hand for attention and continued, "Thank you. I was indeed happy with my result – but guess what I thought about when I was back home again?"

"Were you thinking about what your opponent was going to figure out to improve on your improvement, for the next time you would play each other?" Oliver asked quickly.

"Exactly!" Eduardo replied. "And hard as it is to believe, the story repeated itself. I played the same opponent four different times, every single time I had the dark pieces – I never have played this opponent with me playing the white pieces – and every single game we repeated the same opening moves, with each time my changing up my choice of move at an earlier stage. In fact, the last time I played him, I changed up my move just four moves into the game, just to ensure that I would be the one surprising him instead of him being ready for me! And it worked! I still have a perfect score against this opponent."

Eduardo paused for a little to let the story sink in and then continued. "What I want you to learn from this story is what I simply call 'Always Improve'; the mindset or attitude that anything you do can be improved upon. Always strive to improve, aim for the best you can be, and see what you can do to improve it even more. Never let 'good enough' get in the way of excellence.

"Here's how I would recommend you apply this to being ready for the state championships," he continued, looking around at all the students who were listening carefully. "While I expect you all to continue sharpening your play with the puzzles and training positions, I would like you as a team to look back over the games that you all played in the last state qualifier. Work together to identify in every single game – not just from the games you lost but from every single game – what you would do differently to improve if you had the same position played again.

"While it's fairly obvious to do this for games you've lost, many people miss out on the opportunity to learn and improve from games they've won or drawn. If you will do this, you can indeed build a plan of action in case you face any of the same opponents you've played against recently. Plus, this will help build your confidence in being ready for the state championships."

"Wow, that sounds like a great plan to be ready for state!" Gabe replied. "There's not that much time though. How can we do it efficiently?"

"I can put together a database to track all the games," Cho said. "That way we can all easily see the key positions. We can even store comments in it, so we know exactly what the plans behind the suggested improvements are!"

"That would be great!" Nikolai chimed in. "I can help with inputting the moves into the database."

"How about we sort the games by the ones our team won, drew, or learned," Gabe suggested. "Then let's work through them to identify the key point in each game. If we start by having the person who played the game mark where they think the key point is and one or two suggestions as alternatives, we could then swap games and have a second person review those suggestions, just to make sure we're on the right track before spending too much time going deep into each game."

Eduardo had listened to them work out their plans for tackling this project. "Great work applying 'Better Together,'" the master said with a smile. "I think you've got this. I'll look forward to seeing you at the state championships!"

"Thank you!" everyone on the team said, nearly in unison. "Wow! That was amazing!" Cho said when Eduardo had left the room. "Just when we think that we have it all figured out, there's another revelation of how to get even better, to 'Always Improve.' I'm really excited about putting this into action and being ready for a great showing at state!"

The others all nodded, and they got to work immediately, putting their plan into action.

That evening, back at home, April pulled out the Chart of Champions from behind her closet door and filled in a few additional blanks. As she looked at it on her desk, she thought back to the many lessons she had learned, and how far she had come already. She felt that she had everything she needed and simply needed to apply herself to be ready for the state championships. She just knew she was going to win the scholarship, and along with it open the path for her future college.

CHAPTER 16

THE DAY OF the state championships, April awoke early and lay in bed for a few minutes. She thought back over her journey to this point; how she had trained and prepared and how so many people had helped her along the way. As she thought about the big event that day, her mind leaped forward to imagining herself on stage receiving the scholarship she had dreamed about so often. April shivered with excitement, then jumped out of bed and dressed quickly.

In the kitchen she found her mom frying eggs for breakfast. "Good morning, April," Sara said. "Breakfast is ready, and I'm almost done packing a lunch for you."

"Thanks, Mom," April replied. "I'm not really hungry right now."

"I understand," her mom replied. "You're probably just a little nervous, and that can block hunger. You should eat anyway though. You'll need the energy later."

April managed to eat a little before Cathy pulled up with the school van she had reserved to pick up the team and travel together. "We'll be there to support you later in the afternoon once Michael's baseball playoffs game finishes," Sara said with a wave and a smile. "Have a great time, April – I'm sure you'll do well. Have fun too!"

April smiled and waved goodbye as she stepped into the van. "Good morning!" April said to Cathy. "That's awesome you could get the van with the lift so we all could ride together with Gabe!"

There was a chorus of 'good mornings' as April climbed into the van. But as Cathy drove towards the convention center where the state championships were being held, the team fell silent. Each person was thinking about the tournament about to begin. They all knew they had prepared as best they could, but they still had butterflies in their stomachs as they felt the tension of the championships about to begin.

Finally, Cathy spoke. "Team, we are a few minutes away from the tournament location. I just want to say a few things. First, logistics – I've secured a team room for us, so we'll be able to gather before and after each round easily. This will give you a chance to prep for each round just like Eduardo showed you at the state qualifier. Second, I want you all to know how proud I am of each one of you. You have each made great progress both individually and as a team. I'm very excited for all of you!

"But much more than just for this tournament, I'm excited for each of you in your lives. You've all learned some great skills that as long as you apply them, will allow you to continually improve your results in chess competition. More importantly, these skills are fundamental life skills that, when you apply them to all areas of your life, they will help you achieve in developing each of your unique abilities. As for me, I must add that it is a joy to be a part of your journey."

As Cathy pulled in and parked, she finished, "We have a big day in front of us! Let's now focus on one game, one move at a time. Do your best, and let the results be what they may. Let's be known first for our great sportsmanship, and secondly, as a team that never gives up! Are you ready?"

"Yes!" The team gave a hearty reply and jumped out. They didn't even wait for the lift, and together carried Gabe in his wheelchair to the sidewalk.

"Thank you," Gabe said. "Yay, we're here! Let's go in and win!" Together the team entered the convention center. They walked around at first to figure out where they would be playing. Once they found their team room, they settled in and started playing warm-up games and puzzles.

There was no sense of bravado in the room, just a confident, quiet sense of purpose. They were here to do their best, and they were mentally prepared and ready.

Participants, please make your way to your seats for opening announcements and round one, came the announcement over the PA system. The noise nearly made April jump.

"Ok, let's go!" Gabe called out, and together they headed out to the playing hall which was now nearly packed. It seemed to April that there were at least 500 participants in the room.

After one last round of high-fives, the team separated to find their assigned places, and April made her way over to her seat for the first round.

The announcements continued, "Coaches, parents, siblings, please clear the floor as quickly as you can so that we can begin on time. Participants, please be sure that you are seated at the correct board number."

As the noise in the room settled down, the announcer went on, "Welcome to our state championships! It's a pleasure to see you here. Do you all realize everyone playing in this room today is already a winner by having qualified to be here? Let's give a hand for your achievements so far!"

When the responding applause settled down, he continued with standard reminders of key rules of play, pointed out where the restrooms for the participants were and clarified a few other logistics. Finally, he said, "To signal the start of the first round, we have a special guest."

April saw Eduardo the chess master climb the stairs to the

stage, shake hands with the announcer, then turn to the mic, facing the players.

"Before we begin our games, I would like to thank the event sponsors that make possible some amazing scholarship opportunities," he said. "I'm sure you've all read about these, but just to be sure, I want to mention that we have some very generous scholarships for the grade champions, plus we have for the first time ever, an equally generous scholarship for the top female finisher!"

The players cheered again, and Eduardo waited for the room to quiet down. "It's a pleasure to be here with you all again. Some years ago, I had the honor of competing in this very event. Now, you all are competing for the championship and these scholarships. I would like to remind all of you, however, that there is much more to this event and this game of chess than the prizes here today.

"Chess is indeed like life. There are many ways in which what you learn in playing chess will help you make better decisions in life. It's important to have a goal and a plan in chess – the same in life. It's important to use all your pieces together to achieve your plan – in daily life too, teamwork is important. We are indeed Better Together. Today every game played will involve either winning or losing, or end in a draw. However, every game can be a win if your attitude is to Win, Draw, or Learn!

"I know you are eager to begin, so I'll leave you with just one final thought for now. Chess is unlike life in the sense that chess is a game – you play it, learn from it, and start over to learn more. In life, you have just the one life in front of you. I would encourage each of you to think carefully about your unique abilities, about your goals and plans, so that at the end of your life you can look back with joy on the path you chose."

Eduardo paused, and the room was so quiet you could have heard a pin drop. Then he continued, "Ok, it's time. Let's show respect and sportsmanship at all times. Please keep it quiet while games are in progress. Shake hands and begin!"

April shook hands with her opponent, and the room was silent except for the subdued sounds of hundreds of chess pieces being moved.

April played confidently though carefully, focused intently on her board, avoiding even the slightest temptation to look at games being played on either side. Her many hours of training and practice paid off, as she found herself in a better position right out of the opening moves, found a plan, and pushed through to achieve a winning position. She was about to checkmate her opponent when he extended his hand to resign. She had just won her first game at the state championships!

April was elated as she walked to the team room but kept her emotions in check as she turned her attention immediately towards the next round. She went through the Healthy Habits checklist, drinking water and forcing herself to eat just a little bit of fruit and nuts, stepping outside for two minutes of quick jumping-jacks to get her blood flowing, and then heading back to the team room to be ready for the next round.

The day progressed, and with it, April's confidence and focus. She easily won her second game, as her opponent made a tactical mistake right in the opening which April immediately spotted, pouncing on the opportunity and winning a free bishop, which was an advantage she had no trouble converting into the win.

In the third game of the day she fought hard, and though ending up with a slightly worse position, was able to hang on and force a draw by repeatedly checking her opponent's king. This put her at 2.5 points out of 3 with two rounds to go. Her 4th round opponent was another girl, and this game proved to be her hardest test so far as they were very evenly matched. Near the end, with very few pieces left on the board, April's opponent made one misstep, which was enough for April. She found a series of moves ending with forking her opponent's rook and king with her knight and followed it by promoting a pawn into a queen.

When she finally checkmated her opponent, they shook hands – and April suddenly realized that their game was the last to finish in that round! April made her way back to the team room, quite tired, but feeling exhilarated at the same time. She knew she had just one more game to go. When she arrived in the team room, the rest of the team was there.

"How did you do?" Gabe called out.

As April smiled and gave them a tired thumbs-up, the room burst into a loud cheer!

"Great work, April!" Cho said. "That win puts our team in 1st place in the standings also! Great job!"

Cathy came over and gave April a quick hug. "Nicely done, April! Now get some water and orange slices. No need to discuss the game you just played – there's plenty of time later on to do that. Let's focus on preparing for the final round."

April nodded weakly. She wasn't sure she had the strength for this last game after the previous grueling mental battle, but she was determined to do her best, one move at a time. She drank water, went outside for some fresh air, and then returned to the team room, where she lay down on the floor in a corner and closed her eyes for a few minutes.

CHAPTER 17

A TAP ON HER shoulder woke April.

Cathy was leaning over her, "April, it's time to get ready – the round starts in just twenty minutes, and the team has some info you probably want to know."

April got up and stretched, then joined the rest of the team sitting in a circle talking about the upcoming final round.

Oliver was speaking seriously for once, "Ok, team, it's going to be a very tight finish. We've scored well already, but that is all behind us. Here's what's going on now. Our team sits in first place, but only by half a point. We're going to need at least three wins this final round to have a chance for first place in the team awards. On top of that, with Gabe and Nikolai still on perfect scores, they are going to be facing the toughest competition as they work to try to win the championships both individually as well as for the team. Cho and I are both sitting at three wins, so at least one of us has to win to give our team a good chance. And that leaves the rest up to April."

Cho looked at April as he continued, "I've had a chance to see the pairings posted, and April is up against a strong player – which is to be expected, considering she's already got 3 and a half points out of 4. However, it gets quite interesting here. April's currently sitting in first place for girls." The team interrupted with a cheer, and April smiled.

Cho continued, "The challenge is that there's another girl just half a point back, and if she wins, April's in a 'must win' situation to win the scholarship or at least get a draw to be able to tie for first. On top of that, her opponent this round is the boy who won the state qualifier championships – the one whom Gabe played last round!"

April's confidence suddenly shattered when she heard who she was paired against – the boy who had beaten Gabe! How could she possibly win against him? Besides she felt again how very tired she was after having played four rounds already.

Cathy noticed the change reflected in April's face and walked over to her. "April," she whispered, "remember your dream! Don't give up, April! You can do this! Remember, play the board not the person."

Cathy's words helped, and April slowly felt herself growing in her determination to do her best to win.

Just then Gabe spoke up quietly, "April, remember when we applied the concept of 'Always Improve' to our tournament games?"

April nodded.

"Well," Gabe continued, "when we reviewed my game from the last qualifier against this opponent, we found some interesting possibilities. Take a look at this move here."

While the rest of the team worked through some last-minute prep for their matches, Gabe and April replayed Gabe's game from the prior tournament until they reached the moment Gabe had in mind. "See this?" he said, "Right here, I missed an opportunity. If I had played this other move instead, I would have had a solid position with very good chances of attacking and winning. What do you think?"

April thought about it carefully and replied. "Yes, I see that! Let me give it a try. Let me replay the moves to make sure I've got it."

She quickly replayed the moves from the beginning to that position, and when she had finished, Gabe said with a smile, "You've got it April! I think it will work - at least it's a good try, and you could surprise him with it. You can do it!"

April smiled and said, "Thank you, Gabe!"

He replied, "It's the least I can do. Look, I've got a right arm now thanks to you!" Gabe moved his Robotic Arm up and down as he spoke.

April smiled at his cheerful action.

"Ok team – quick huddle, and time to focus!" Cathy called out. The team gathered in a circle, closed their eyes, and, following Cathy's direction, breathed deeply a few times, blowing it out slowly, focusing on the moves that they would be playing in just a minute.

As the team left the room together, they high-fived again with Cathy and with each other. Anyone watching them could tell that this team was out to do their absolute best – they were determined. As the team made their way to the playing hall, April saw her Dad near the entrance, scanning the crowd coming in. She ran up to him, "Dad, I'm so glad you made it! Are the others here too?" "Yes, we all made it. I saw the standings – you are doing great!

I know you can do it!" he said as he gave her a quick hug. "Thanks, Dad! I'll do my best," April said, and headed into the hall, making her way towards the front of the room.

As she got closer, she saw her opponent already sitting at the board, chatting with someone at the next board. He appeared confident. When April arrived and sat down, he looked at her a little in surprise, and said: "Are you sure this is where you're playing?"

April simply nodded, sat down, and filled out her scoresheet to be ready to write down her moves. She was going to focus only on the moves, ignoring anything her opponent might do or say that could distract her. She did see, however, that just a couple boards away was another girl – likely the one that was just behind her in the standings.

When the round began, April made her moves very slowly.

Even though she knew the moves she was planning to play, she didn't want her opponent to think that she had it planned out. Her opponent moved quickly and confidently, and a couple of times even stood up while April was thinking, wandering off and looking at the top boards to see how those games were progressing.

With her king castled into safety, having brought out all her back row of pieces, they were nearing the moment where Gabe had found an improvement. April played slowly until the critical moment came. Her heart beat fast as she wondered if her opponent would play the same move he had played against Gabe.

He did! Apparently thinking that he was simply repeating what had worked before, he played the move again rather quickly, but this time April responded immediately with the improvement that Gabe had found.

April's opponent was surprised at her sudden move, looked at the board a little puzzled, and then sunk into deep thought. April just sat quietly, thinking about what she had looked at before the game and the plan that was part of this surprise move. Her opponent glanced up at her a couple of times, suddenly aware that perhaps he had been drawn into a planned sequence of moves. He frowned, took a sip of water, put his head in his hands, and stared at the position for nearly 20 minutes. When he finally moved, it was indeed one of the moves that Gabe had foreseen, and April was prepared with her next move which she also played confidently.

Again, he sunk into deep thought, respect for April's skill now showing on his face as he dug in to try to find a way to escape the threats forming around his king.

April got up to use the restroom, and on her way back noticed that the other girl was finished. She took a quick look at the results chart and noted that the girl had won. That meant she had to win! This other girl was now ahead of April with four wins out of five. April made her way back to her board and sat down, determined to find the best moves and win the game.

The game continued, this time with both players taking their time very carefully on every move, knowing that just one slight misstep would likely prove the turning point.

April's opponent defended well. He found the only move out several times to block April's attack, but April didn't give up. She kept searching for a way to make her plan of attack work.

Finally, they reached another critical moment. April's opponent captured one of April's rooks with his rook, and April prepared to recapture. She had a couple of choices. She could take with her king, leaving her king slightly exposed but still with chances to attack, or she could recapture with her bishop. April quickly realized that taking with her bishop would be a big mistake – it lost protection of a key square near her king, so she would have to recapture with her king.

Rather than making the move right away, April started thinking further ahead. After she would recapture with her king, her opponent would probably play his queen over checking her king, and she would have to move away. April continued calculating, but try as she might, she couldn't find a clear way to force a win. She thought she would have a slightly better position, but she wanted more, so she 'dug in' and started thinking even more deeply. She spent more than 20 minutes to find a couple possible ways to gain an advantage – but she also felt that it could very well end in a draw.

A little frustrated that she was unable to find a clear win after she felt she had such a good attack going, April thought for a moment about her dream and her determination to win the scholarship, and she suddenly turned back to the board determined to fight harder even if it meant taking a few risks. She decided that taking with the king wasn't good enough and recaptured the rook with her bishop.

As April completed the move, her opponent looked up at her with a look of complete surprise on his face, then moved his knight onto the square now left undefended by the bishop, checking April's king and at the same time forking her queen!

April had blundered with nearly the worst possible mistake, and she was going to lose her queen. April looked, stunned by what she saw on the board, unable to comprehend how she could have blundered so badly. As she stared, her eyes filled with tears, and she heard her opponent say very softly, "I'm sorry…"

April just sat staring at the position, until the reality sunk in, then she finally started thinking about what she could do to try to save the position – but it was completely hopeless. In just one move she had gone from a promising position to a completely lost position. April finally made a move, her opponent took her queen, and though April still tried to put up a defense, there was nothing she could really do, and he checkmated her king just a few moves later.

As they shook hands after the game, again he said, "I'm really sorry. You played amazingly well and almost had me. You have some real talent!"

April walked out slowly; she was hardly able to see because of the tears she was fighting to hold back.

Her dad met her at the door of the playing hall, and one look at April's face told him what had happened. He put his arm around April's shoulders and silently walked with her outside of the convention center. When they were outside, April could hold it in no longer and burst out crying.

Her dad just let her cry with her head on his shoulder, giving her a gentle hug, and whispered, "It's okay, April. Your mom and I are so very proud of you."

April slowly stopped sobbing. "But Dad, I was so close! I wanted to win the scholarship! I failed when I tried out for the soccer team, now I've failed at this also. I'm afraid I won't ever make it to university!"

Suddenly he understood. "April," he said, putting both his hands on her shoulders and looking into her eyes, "do you mean that you tried out for soccer just because you hoped to get to university on a scholarship? And then you tried chess for the same reason?"

April just nodded, the tears coming again.

"Oh, April!" her dad said, giving her a hug again, "Whatever made you worry so about not being able to go to university?"

"Well, I overheard you and Mom talking one night. I had gotten up to use the bathroom – you were saying that you were worried about whether it would work for me to go to university," April replied slowly.

"Ahhh, I see," Davis replied, then continued earnestly, "Look April, your mom and I love you and your brothers unconditionally – whether you go to university or not. And just because I didn't get the raise I was expecting back then, you never know – it may come around again in time. Really, please don't worry. We are very proud of you and what you've done. Look at what you did for Gabe! I've seen him using his Robotic Arm so well; it's as if he was born with it!"

"Thank you, Dad," April replied, giving her Dad another long hug. "That helps – but it still hurts."

"I understand," Davis replied.

"Let's go back and see how the rest of the team did. I hope that they pulled through despite my loss." April said.

Together they went back to the team room, where they found the rest of the team congratulating Gabe, who had just come back from winning his final round! He was going to be at least co-champion of the tournament.

April went up to him to congratulate him, and before she could speak, Gabe said, "April, I know how much you wanted to win, but I want you to know that you've already won – at least when it comes to life! You've helped me so very much with your generosity and kindness."

April hugged Gabe and shed a few tears, but wiped them away

quickly and said "Congratulations, Gabe – I'm really happy for you! How is our team doing?"

"Cho went to check on the remaining games," Gabe replied. "It's very close, especially as Nikolai is playing someone from our main competition for the team awards."

Just then Cho came into the room. "Well, team," he said, "it's down to the very last game! If Nikolai can pull this win off, we've secured first place for teams! If he draws or loses, we'll end up top 5, but not sure what spot exactly."

Cathy entered the room just then and spotted April.

She came over and said while hugging her, "April, I've been looking for you – I heard how your game went. How are you feeling? I feel so badly for you after all the effort that you put in – I thought you were going to win this one!"

April fought back the tears again but managed to say quietly, "It's okay, Cathy. It was so close – I did my best but made a blunder eventually. For now, I just hope that Nikolai can win and help our team take first. If I had only won, we would already have secured the title." A few tears came again, and April turned towards the corner to wipe her eyes.

"Let's go to the playing hall to meet Nikolai when he finishes," Oliver suggested.

"Good idea!" Cathy said, and they all made their way to the exit from the main playing hall. As they arrived, the door opened, and Nikolai came through. He saw them and immediately gave a 'thumbs up'!

"Hurray!" April couldn't help herself. "We took first!!"

The team went back to the team room to celebrate taking first on total team score plus Gabe and Nikolai sharing first place for individual scores with a third player (all having achieved a perfect five points).

April enjoyed going on stage with the team to receive the first-place team award which included a plaque for each of the team players, and the crowd cheered loudly as the team together lifted Gabe and his wheelchair on and off the stage, both with the team and when he went up to receive his first place co-champion award. Still, she had a hard time holding back the tears again when the scholarships were announced, and the girl she had seen playing just a couple boards away from her went up to receive the prize.

That night, April lay awake in bed long after her usual time to fall asleep. She kept replaying over and over in her mind the position where she had blundered. Finally, she spoke to herself rather sternly, "Stop it, April! Win, Draw, or Learn! Look, you already came so far, just think about all the good progress you've made. Just stop thinking about what could have been, and instead think about all you've learned and can still learn from this. It's a game, and today is just one more step in the game of life." It helped a little, and she finally fell asleep, though even in sleep, she dreamed about chess positions and struggling to find the best move.

CHAPTER 18

THE NEXT WEEK April was busy preparing for finals and didn't touch a chessboard. She poured herself into her homework and prep for the tests and even thought she would skip going to chess club where she had been a regular for much of the school year.

Cathy noticed April's absence from chess club when the club gathered for the year-end celebration and went to find her.

April was in the library studying when Cathy finally found her. "April, aren't you coming to chess club? It's our last meeting of the year, and there is a special focus on the chess team's first-place finish."

"I don't know," April replied. "I'm busy preparing for finals." "I know," Cathy said, "and I'm sure that last game is still painful – but you really are a big part of the team and one of the reasons the team came in first this year. They all will miss you if you don't come."

"Well, okay," April replied slowly. "I'll come now."

When April entered the room, the chess club let out a cheer. They had their party together, with pizza that Cathy ordered in, and when they were finally wrapping up, Cathy made one more announcement.

"Chess team, it's been such a pleasure seeing your progress this year! You've all done well, whether winning or learning, and you've really shown that indeed we are all 'better together.' I'm really proud of this whole team, not just for your chess results, but more for who you have all become." Cathy then added, "Please remember to be on time for the all-school assembly next week Friday, right after finals. I understand that the principal would like to recognize the chess team at the assembly."

April continued to focus on her prep for finals, determined that at least her grades would be her best ever even though her dream of winning the chess scholarship that year had been dashed. She tried to forget about what could have been and stayed focused on the exams. Once she completed the last final, April had time to reflect on what had happened that school year, and by the time Friday came, she was in good spirits again.

On Friday, April arrived early at the assembly and looked for Cathy. She found her talking quietly to the principal, so April waited until they were finished.

Once Cathy was free, and the principal turned to talk with someone else, April approached her.

"How are you doing, April? It's good to see you." Cathy said.

"I'm doing well," April replied. "I've been too busy with finals to think much about how I had really counted on winning that scholarship." April's voice quavered just a little.

April continued, "I've come to realize something though."

"Yes?" Cathy asked.

April continued, "Well, I've had a chance to think about this whole year, and I realize that I've learned so much along the way, that I've already succeeded. You've helped me gain a whole new perspective on life. I've realized that I'm not a victim of circumstances – also that going to university is something that I really do want to achieve. Now it is a goal of mine – it's no longer just a dream.

"In some ways, I feel that I was pinning my hopes completely on winning the scholarship to help me get there, whereas I see now that I can apply what I learned during this chess journey to put a plan together. With all the friends that I've come to know and appreciate through this chess journey, I really do believe it will be possible someday. We are indeed 'better together,' and I know that if I'm stuck somewhere, Gabe, Cho, and many others are eager to help where possible.

"Whether it's through a chess scholarship or some other way, and whatever happens, I do believe that I'll continue to Win, Draw, and Learn along the way. And you know what? I think my favorite part of the whole year in chess club wasn't even chess – it was surprising Gabe with the Robotic Arm!" April smiled as she finished. Cathy smiled also and gave April another hug. "I am so very happy to hear you say this, April. You are just beginning to discover your talents, and I do believe your future is very bright. Just like you learned from Gabe – it's not money, things, or what we see on the outside that matters. What's inside is most important. And you," Cathy paused for effect, "you, April, have a very bright future where I believe you'll be able to have a tremendous positive impact on those around you."

As the assembly began, April looked around the room and was both surprised and pleased to see her parents among the family members who had come for this final assembly. Her dad rarely took time off work, yet here he was – and her Mom being a school teacher never took time off during these final days of the school year. She figured they must have come to support her, knowing how disappointed she had been about not winning the scholarship, and waved and smiled when she thought they were looking her direction.

The assembly continued as it usually did, with recognition for teachers, achievements by the various clubs, and the presentation of various awards including several sizable scholarships. April was not surprised at all when Michael received a robotics scholarship.

When it was time for the chess team to be recognized, they gathered at the front of the room while the principal took a few minutes to talk about how pleased he was with seeing the team represent the school, returning with not only a couple of individual champions but also the first-place team trophy. The crowd applauded and cheered, and as the team started to move back towards their seats, she saw Cathy talking to Gabe quietly for a moment. April went over there, intending to congratulate Gabe once more on his championship plus his sizable scholarship for his efforts when Cathy straightened up and looked around the room for someone.

When she spied April heading their way, Cathy called her. "April, do you mind staying here with Gabe for a few minutes?"

"Sure," April replied, puzzled by the request.

She walked on over to Gabe, who was sitting in his chair with a smile on his face.

"Do you know why Cathy asked me to stay here with you?" April asked Gabe.

"Hmm, I wonder," Gabe replied with a twinkle in his eye. "Remember when we first met? Here, want to shake hands?"

April nearly laughed as Gabe reached out this time with his Robotic Arm, stretching it over his head at a hilarious angle.

April turned her attention back to the principal as he held up his hand and the room grew quiet. When the room was completely quiet, the principal spoke. "Students and friends, and family members, I have a special announcement to make. As you have all seen, this year has been a good year indeed. Our school has been making special efforts to encourage involvement in STEM-related activities, and the results of our robotics, as well as our chess team, speak highly about the success of these endeavors."

He paused as the audience cheered again, and then continued. "Today I have the pleasure of announcing a new scholarship award that was added just this year, worth nearly one full year of college tuition to an in-state private college of the recipient's choice. This award will be given annually and is determined by a panel of judges that vote on all entries for this scholarship. It is awarded to the most innovative STEM-related project that has a social benefit.

After careful consideration of a number of qualified applicants, our judges have come to a decision. The winner of this scholarship goes to a member of our winning chess team for excellent work taking a Robotic Arm and figuring out a way to pair this device with other technologies to help one of her chess team members navigate life better. Please help me congratulate April!"

The room erupted in loud cheers while April just stood, not believing what she was hearing. Scholarship? Her?

The principal looked towards her and motioned for her to come forward. April walked towards him, thinking she was dreaming and shook hands with the principal as he handed her a certificate with the scholarship.

The rest of the assembly was a blur she could hardly remember later – congratulations from Gabe and her chess team members, her parents coming up and giving her big hugs, Cathy coming over and, with a hint of tears in her own eyes, beaming as she congratulated April. Pictures were taken afterward, and once the assembly was dismissed, the principal came to April and asked her to come to his office for a few minutes.

When she arrived, there were two men in his office dressed in business suits who congratulated her on the scholarship and handed her their cards. April looked at the cards and was surprised to see that the men were from the top private university in her home state, known for its focus on technology! The two men said that they had seen the Robotic Arm and had heard from Gabe about the story of how it was made to work for him; they hoped that April would be willing to consider the college they represented.

The university representatives said they would be happy to help her apply for additional scholarships. They mentioned that based on her grades over the next couple of years, there was even the possibility of a full-ride scholarship as the university was focusing on encouraging more women to pursue STEM careers.

That night after dinner dishes were cleared away, April's family sat around the table talking about the amazing surprise of the day when a thought suddenly struck April.

"I'm puzzled, though," April said. "The principal said that this scholarship was awarded based on all the entries – I never thought of even entering. Do you have any idea who entered the Robotic Arm in the STEM scholarship competition?"

"I don't know," Michael replied. "How about you ask Gabe? Maybe he knows since he had the arm they would have had to inspect."

"Well, sleuths," Sara spoke up. "I guess you'll find out sooner or later, but your dad had a hand in this."

April looked at her dad in surprise, "You submitted the entry, Dad?"

"Guilty as charged," he replied with a smile. "When I saw what you were doing with the Robotic Arm, and how much you wanted to help Gabe, I felt sure that you had a chance of winning, so I went ahead and entered it. I asked Gabe not to let on though, as I didn't want to get your hopes up in case it didn't work out."

"Oh, Dad!" April jumped up and gave her Dad a big hug and kissed him on the cheek. "I don't think I can thank you enough for doing that! I had no idea until it happened!"

Davis replied, "Well, I'm very happy that it worked out, April. And really, you worked so hard for your scholarship; you do deserve this – even if it isn't the chess scholarship you were hoping to win! I've got a feeling that you may find a future in this STEM field. Who knows, maybe you'll even someday be producing products that the company I work for will market!"

"I don't know about that," April replied "but I am so very grateful to everyone. In fact, I think this has been the best year I can remember! It has been the hardest in some ways, but best also. I feel as if I've learned so much about the attitudes of success in life, something I value even more than winning the scholarship."

CHAPTER 19

MONTHS LATER....

"Hey, April, can you spare a minute?"

April slowed her brisk pace as Teegan's question interrupted her thoughts about the meeting she was going to be having shortly.

"Yes, of course, what can I do for you?" April replied with a smile and a quick hug.

The relationship between Teegan and April had certainly changed. Since the day of April's STEM Scholarship award, Teegan seemed to have developed a newly discovered respect and appreciation for April and her talents, and while she still had witty comments to make occasionally, no longer were they cutting. Perhaps some of the change in Teegan was rubbing off from April. It was not unusual for her to come to April for input on one topic or another.

"Could we meet up sometime when we can talk?" Teegan asked. "Sure, what's up?" April replied.

"I've just been chosen captain of the soccer team – "

"Good for you!" exclaimed April.

"Thanks!" Teegan smiled. "Well, there are a few challenges we've got, and I've got to figure out how best to address them all. Like, for one thing, I think our team could be working better together. Anyway, I thought that you might be able to give me some suggestions."

"I'll be happy to if I can," April replied.

"Great!" Teegan went on, "it seems that we lose games we should win. It's like our team doesn't believe they are as good as I think they are!"

April smiled, "It sounds to me as if they need to develop the Can-Do Attitude as a team!"

"Okay, what do you mean by that?" Teegan asked. "Is that something you maybe could come to a team meeting and talk about?"

"Yes, perhaps I can," replied April. "What time do you practice?" "Thursdays we have practice after school. Could you make that?" Teegan replied.

"Yes, I'll be there," April replied. "Looking forward to helping out!"

✦

April's life was busier than ever this school year. She was a key member of the expanding chess team, attending the Robotics club, and now working with Cathy to get her latest initiative off the ground. It seemed as if every day had more to do than she could accomplish. At the same time, April had never felt more joyful.

"Are you ready?" Cathy asked as she met April just outside the principal's office.

"Yes, I'm excited!" April replied with a smile.

"Good! I think it will be best if you take the lead and start this off. I think he's going to be quite supportive." Cathy said brightly just before they entered the principal's office which doubled as a small meeting room.

"Happy to see you today!" the principal greeted them as he stood up to shake hands. "I must say that I've been looking forward to hearing more ever since Cathy said that you had an initiative you wanted to propose that could significantly increase the already positive trends we see in test scores."

"Thank you," April replied and dove right into the topic. "You see, last year in school I experienced something life-changing. Cathy introduced me to a few people, and through learning the game of chess, my whole world feels like it's completely changed – in a good way that is!" She said with a little chuckle.

"I would think so," the principal replied with a smile. "What with joining the chess team, qualifying for the state chess championships, winning the STEM scholarship, and ending the year with nearly straight A's on your final scorecard, I would think so!"

April blushed slightly at the words of praise. "Well, there is even more happening," she continued. "Several other students in school have come to me to ask for help with various challenges they are experiencing. For example, my friend Teegan, captain of the soccer team this year."

The principal nodded, "Please continue."

April went on. "I had this idea which Cathy encouraged me to bring to you. Through competing in chess, I've learned a number of things. Through trying to win the chess scholarship but failing, then being awarded the STEM scholarship, I realized something. What I learned while trying to improve in chess helped me win the STEM scholarship – so it wasn't really about chess itself so much as what I learned while studying the game that has helped me."

"Please go on," the principal said as he leaned forward listening intently.

"Well, here's the idea. What if we could create a new club called something like 'Champions by Choice.' I imagine that each month we would have a guest or member of the club share about a fundamental life skill, how they learned it, and what difference it has made for them. Each member of this club would receive something I received from Cathy last year – a life skills chart called the Chart of Champions. We could use this tool to do a self-assessment and to measure progress."

"I know that we can learn these life skills while learning chess, so I was thinking we would all learn and play chess, focusing on understanding and developing these skills. At the same time, we could be intentionally looking at how these life skills help us succeed in school."

"Let me stop you for a moment. I like what I hear of the concept; however, why form a separate club from our current chess club?" the principal asked. "Have you thought about simply integrating these ideas into the regular club meetings?"

April answered, "The way I envision it, while we would all learn and practice some chess, there would not be any expectations of members becoming high-level chess players. In fact, if students wanted to pursue chess, they would be expected to join the chess club to train and join the chess team. The purpose of chess in the club I'm thinking of would be to leverage all the life skills that are illustrated and developed so well through the game, just like I learned," April replied.

"You see," April continued, rising to her feet in her enthusiasm as she spoke, "the main goal in the club would be to help everyone in the club grow and develop to the point of being 'champions' in terms of life skills."

"Just imagine a growing number of students," Cathy added, "eventually a majority of students in this school, developing 'Can-Do Attitudes,' working 'Better Together,' and treating failures as simply 'Learning' – plus showing 'Respect' for everyone? The word 'Champion' really doesn't need to imply that because one is first, others are therefore behind."

"With this concept, each student is striving and growing to become the champion that each one has the potential to be," April said. "Can you just imagine what would happen to test scores and attendance if more and more students grew and developed the 'champion by choice' mindsets?"

April sat down, a little surprised by her boldness.

The principal sat for a minute and gave a slight nod to Cathy. He turned his gaze back to April, considering, and after a moment spoke. "April, I appreciate you sharing this idea. As you say, the possible outcomes are very attractive. I'm not sure that this idea will take root as quickly as I'm sure you hope it will, but there is no denying the transformation we've seen in you. I will be happy to provide official support and endorsement for this initiative, provided that you take the lead and Cathy is willing to be the club advisor. We can give it a one-year trial."

"Thank you," April said. "I'm quite confident that the results will be positive, at least if we can accomplish anything like the experience I've had so far."

"And," the principal smiled and said as he stood up to shake hands, "I think that you have what it takes to make this work. While I need to give it time to measure results, I do have confidence that you will make a positive impact."

As they left the principal's office, Cathy spoke. "April, I'm really, really proud of you for taking the initiative on this. You've grown tremendously over the last year, and now you're stepping out to use what you have to expand a good influence and help even more become Champions, just like you have become."

"Thank you," April said. "I want you to know how grateful I am that you took an interest in me and invested the time to help me grow. Now I'm so excited to see others receive similar opportunities."

"I know," April continued, more to herself than to Cathy, "I think I'll invite Teegan and the soccer team to join the Champions by Choice with the first club meeting. And I'll see if Gabe is willing to be my first presenter too."

Later that day as they gathered around the dinner table, April shared about her meeting with the principal. When she finished, her dad said with a smile, "This is great, April! I'm really happy to hear of your plans for Champions by Choice."

The family talked together for a while, discussing the new club and what could be accomplished through it. When the conversation started to slow down, her mother said, "Well, this is all certainly great and exciting to hear. But now I've started wondering when your Dad is going to share his good news!"

"What is it, Dad?" the siblings said in unison and looked at their father.

"Did you get the promotion?" April guessed.

Davis nodded. "Today I received good news! I'm being asked to take on an even better role than I was expecting. They've asked me to take a lead management role in building out a STEM product line. The robotics line of products I've been handling is just one of many product lines I'll now be overseeing." Davis replied.

"Oh wow, that's awesome!" Michael exclaimed. "Can't wait to see some of the cool stuff you'll be working with!"

"Maybe you'll bring home another toy like the Robotic Arm that April can use to help someone else," Max added.

CHAPTER 20

THREE YEARS LATER, the Champions by Choice Club (or CCs as the members called themselves) had grown rapidly, perhaps because of April's ability to recruit nearly every school club leader and sports team captain. April's own story paired with Gabe's use of his Robotic Arm might have been the secret. Whatever it was, the school was experiencing a steady rise in test scores along with a similar drop in absences.

The principal tried to identify the underlying cause, but it was difficult to find conclusive data. Was it related to the continually growing popularity in STEM clubs and programs? Was it perhaps related to the growing numbers of girls involved in the CC and other STEM clubs? While boys still outnumbered the girls in STEM programs, it was no longer as lopsided as it once was. When he analyzed the data filtered by club, no anomalies stood out, with perhaps the exception of the CC.

When Cathy showed up in his office one day during the summer as he puzzled over what the primary cause behind the improved scores could be, he even forgot to say 'hello' and simply said: "So how do you explain this?"

Cathy laughed. "Well, perhaps you can tell me what you are referring to, and then I might be able to answer!"

"Oh, I'm sorry! I didn't even say 'hello' I was so busy thinking about this puzzle," the principal said. He continued, "Our test scores are up, absences are steadily going down, yet when I look at the data, I'm having trouble tracking it back to anyone definitive program or dataset. While the scores in the Champions by Choice Club are indeed higher than the average, is that really because of the club, or because the club attracts those that score well already? Any thoughts?"

Cathy listened carefully then replied slowly, "Perhaps it's a bit of the 'chicken and the egg' question. Difficult to tell what came first, and perhaps knowing the answer is not even that critical. Could it be that the changes happening, such as the Champions by Choice club, are building a mindset that is resulting in a cultural shift? Then the cultural shift raises the mindset of the group as a whole? Somewhat like the sea rising lifts all boats."

"I suppose that could be," the principal replied thoughtfully. "Either way, I'm pleased to see the outcomes happening here!"

"Well, I suspect you didn't come here to listen to me," he smiled. "What is it that I can do for you today, Cathy?"

"I'm here to let you know that I'll be leaving the school shortly," Cathy replied.

"Leaving? Why? You've been making a difference around here!" the principal exclaimed.

Cathy smiled "It seems to me you may have used a different phrase for my work a few years ago."

The principal laughed. "Yes, you're probably right. But I think I've grown as well these last few years, and I've become quite a fan of STEM, mentorship, and a few other concepts I have to say I didn't understand the value of a few years ago. But please explain, why are you thinking of leaving?"

"I'm not thinking of leaving," Cathy replied "I'm actually leaving. You see, I think one of the key factors behind this school's progress is simply you."

The principal looked surprised at Cathy's words.

Cathy continued, "You have been open-minded, you have shown innovative leadership in carefully taking what others would consider risks and in exploring what can be done to continually improve here. You're on a path that I wouldn't be surprised if you win 'best school' in the district if not the state in the next year or two!"

"Why, thank you very much, Cathy! That means a lot hearing such words from you," the principal said, obviously touched by Cathy's words.

"I've been thinking for quite a while. Imagine if what is happening right here in your school was replicated throughout not just the district but also throughout the state and perhaps even our country. What an impact that would have! Imagine the outcome! Besides, with my husband retired, we've wanted to travel more. We think we can align both objectives," Cathy continued.

"Sounds like you'll be busier than ever if you go that route. What do you have in mind?" the principal asked.

Cathy replied brightly. "I plan to visit many other countries as well as travel around our own country, everywhere taking a look at the education systems, discovering even more of what works in various places, as well as sharing the story of this school everywhere we go. Besides, I don't want to get bored."

"I don't think there's any danger of that happening anytime soon!" The principal laughed, and then added, "You know, Cathy, I never imagined I would say this, but I'm going to miss your presence here. You've done a wonderful thing for the students and this community."

"Thank you," Cathy replied. "Feel free to reach out anytime."

Then she added with a smile, "And who knows, I may check back in with some more radical ideas I pick up in traveling."

"Before I wrap things up here, I'll be seeing Gabe back to college – he's starting his 3rd year already. It's quite exciting to see April joining Gabe at the same college too – both on full-ride scholarships! Can you believe it? Based on current trends and my confidence in your leadership, I expect to see many more such students coming from this school."

"Thank you once again, Cathy. I truly am grateful for what you have done here. Best wishes on your new adventure!" the principal said as they shook hands.

CHAPTER 21

AFEW WEEKS LATER, Cathy drove Gabe back to college. When they arrived on campus, as arranged, April and her parents were there to greet them. April saw them arrive and came running over to hug Gabe. "Hi, Gabe! Isn't it exciting that we are going to be together for the next two years? I'm almost all settled into my dorm already. Still, need to finish registering for classes, but I'll be happy to help carry anything you need!"

"Thanks, April," Gabe replied. "Though I've been getting along very well thanks to my Robotic Arm. I'm sure glad you got the scholarship too! It will be great to be back on the chess team together again! By the way, I'll be happy to show you around."

Gabe added, "So when do we launch the Champions by Choice club here?"

April laughed. "How about tomorrow?"

"Sounds good! Well, let's finish getting you registered so we can start," Gabe replied.

Cathy waited along with April's parents as Gabe saw April through completing her registration and a few other details associated with getting settled in.

"It sure is neat to see the friendship between those two," Sara said.

"Yes indeed. They are such good friends and knowing how

they've grown and blossomed over the years, I've got a feeling they are going to make quite a positive impact here just like they did in high school," Cathy replied. "In fact, I've already heard some very good feedback about the chess team that Gabe launched in his freshman year here and how it's grown steadily, becoming a college championship contender. Now with April joining, I have a feeling the team may be taking home the title soon."

Davis was silent, watching and thinking about how grown-up April had suddenly become. When April came back from getting her college ID, Davis went to her. "April, we'll be heading back soon. Can we talk a minute?"

"Sure, Dad! And thank you so much for coming to see me get settled in," April replied, hugging him.

Her dad held her closely for a minute, then spoke, his voice emotional. "April, do you remember that time you overheard your mom and me talking about your future?"

"Yes," April replied, remembering.

He continued, "Look how different things are now! I'm just so very thankful and proud of who you are, of how you use your unique abilities to help others." Davis' voice cracked a little. He paused, then recovered and continued.

"April, I am sure that you will face many new things here at college, and likely some challenges as well. However, I'm confident that you will do well. Just know that you can always call us any time."

"Thank you, Dad! I appreciate what you and Mom have done for me. I'll be sure to keep you updated on how things go."

"You're welcome, April. I love you!" Davis kissed her lightly on the cheek.

"I love you too, Dad," April replied as she returned the kiss and gave him one more hug.

After waving goodbye to April's parents, Gabe showed April all around campus, ending at his favorite corner of the cafeteria. As they ate lunch together and chatted about the upcoming year of studies, Gabe bumped his fork onto the floor.

April moved to pick it up, but before she could do so, Gabe had extended his robotic arm, deftly picking it up and placing it back on the table.

"Thanks to you, I can now do that," he said with a smile. "Wow, that reminded me of when I first met you," April said.

"Remember when you dropped the chess piece, and I picked it up for you? Back when you used to tease me all the time about shaking hands!" April laughed. "Do you still do that?"

"Sometimes, though not so often," Gabe said. "I thought you might be interested in what I'm planning to go into after college."

"What is it?" April asked eagerly.

"Well, the Robotic Arm opened my eyes to a lot of things," Gabe said. "My first couple years here have given me a pretty good idea of what I want to do. I've been thinking a lot about helping others who have it even more difficult than myself. For example, I've heard of a few people who are paralyzed from their neck down – they can only move their eyes and mouth, nothing else. So, I've been thinking about utilizing what I'm learning to explore the possibilities of a system that is completely independent of any physical necessity for operating – simply voice activated. Functions like arms and hands will be trained or programmed to fulfill any task the operator wishes. What do you think?"

"I think that's great!" April said. "Perhaps I can even join you in figuring it out once I get a few years in!"

"That would be awesome, April!" Gabe said. "Just think – 'better together' once again!"

THE END

ACKNOWLEDGMENTS

'Better Together' is one of the life skills that April learns in her journey - and truly applying this concept has been a key to finishing this book. I will almost certainly be leaving someone out who deserves mention here - please accept my apology if I forgot to mention you - it was not intentional - there are many friends who have contributed in various ways to moving this book from idea to reality.

Thank-you to the many students I have had the privilege of working with, sharing struggles & triumphs, whose lives are represented in this story. You have been a primary inspiration for this book.

Thank-you Jeff Rogers (founder of One Accord Partners) for introducing me to Bryan Heathman, founder of Made for Success Publishing.

Thank you, Bryan, DeeDee, and the team at Made for Success Publishing that has made the potentially arduous journey of writing and publishing this book a joy. Bryan, your step by step guidance was just what I needed. In chess, I expect students to trust the guidance that comes from a Chess Master's experience coaching 10,000+ students. Writing this book, I found myself the student, Bryan, the 'Master,' and I cannot thank him enough for all his help along the way. Just as April discovers, having a dream is not enough - Planning and Goal Setting are essential - and in the game of publishing, Bryan is a masterful guide towards achieving the dream.

Thank you to my sister Johanna - you always have and do believe in me, care deeply, and selflessly do whatever you can to help your brothers. In this endeavor as well, you were a tremendous help in proofing, suggesting edits, and giving the feedback that helped make this book move from very rough to so much more polished.

Mallory O'Neill, Thank you for your reading/reviewing/suggesting edits so graciously. Your perspective helped indeed throughout the editing process.

Thank you to the team at Chess4Life who believe in the vision and live out many aspects of this story on a daily basis while interfacing with thousands of students every week - you are a big part of the inspiration for this book and the joy that comes from seeing lives positively impacted.

Thank you to my wife Camilla and children who have given up time so Daddy can 'help others.' Special mention to Caleb, my eldest son to whom I promised the first copy, and at 6 years old he offered to buy it if needed with his own hard-earned $$.

Thank you to my parents who introduced my siblings and me to the wonderful game of chess, sacrificing much to give us the opportunity. I am grateful for all I've learned from their example as they lived out 'never give up' and 'do your best.'

Thank you most of all to my heavenly Father Who gave me not only meaning in this life, but also the promise of eternal life in the next, plus my own unique abilities now dedicated to investing for the good of others.

APPENDIX:

Life Skills Application

For each of the below life skills, consider something that stood out to you in April's journey, then reflect on the application suggestions. Visit elliottneff.com for a printable Chart of Champions template plus additional resources for personal or group discussion.

Can Do Attitude

In what areas do you have a "Can Do Attitude"? What areas do you possibly have a "*Can't Do Attitude*" currently? Consider asking those who know you best for their thoughts (family, coworkers, classmates, friends) Just imagine for a moment "What if…" you could do whatever it is that you want or feel you 'can't.' Imagine the possibilities. Dream Big!

Goal Setting

List 10 goals and analyze them using Cathy's SMART definition. Look for any patterns (maybe you are choosing achievable goals, but are forgetting to define a unit of measurement). What's your main takeaway from this activity? Note that for a *goal* to be meaningful, it is important to connect with the accomplishment of the goal emotionally. Imagine having accomplished the goal - what does it feel like? Imagine it fully!

Healthy Habits

Make a list of some of your current habits that you consider to be GREAT habits to have. What additional habits would you like to form that could help you achieve your goals?

Did you list some habits you would like to be rid of? Try thinking of a new habit that if developed would reduce or eliminate the 'bad habit' you want to get rid of. What ONE habit will you work on developing first?

Respect

Name one or a couple of people you have the highest 'respect' for. What characteristics led to your giving them that level of respect (valuing them)? Think of someone whom you have 'looked down on' or 'devalued' (respect the person's privacy by not naming them publicly). What caused you to have 'low respect' for the person? Can you now try to think of something about the person that you appreciate or value? Do you see how doing this can help build 'respect' for others?

Regarding objects - if objects had feelings, would they 'feel' valued by you?

Focus

Do you find yourself switching from one thing to another frequently, rarely able to maintain concentration on one project for more than a few minutes? How would improving your ability to focus help you? One way to build your ability to focus is to take an activity (chess, music, reading, meditating, etc.) and set a timer to see how long you can stay focused. Keep a journal of how long you stay focused, each time striving to increase it incrementally.

Win. Draw. Learn.

What are some of your 'best wins' in life? What are some of your 'biggest losses'? What did you learn from the losses? Try to find at least one good thing that has or could come out of each loss. Can you share a loss that actually turned out to be very good for you later on, but at the moment felt terrible?

Planning

Choose one of your goals (see Goal Setting). What obstacles do you see preventing the goal from being accomplished? Determine a strategy to overcome each obstacle. What else is necessary in order to accomplish the goal? What actions do you anticipate will lead to accomplishing the goal? What is the first action that would move you towards your goal?

Sportsmanship

Give examples of the best and worst sportsmanship you have experienced or heard of. What stands out to you from these examples? Consider the various situations or groups in which you interact with others (Examples: school, family, work, church, sports) What can you do to be a better sport towards those you interact with?

Never Give Up

Can you share an example of a time when you felt like giving up on something but kept going, and the outcome was better than if you had given up? If not a personal example, consider sharing a story you've heard about someone else never giving up. What in your life are you tempted to quit or give up on because it's hard? Consider applying the following mindsets to your situation: Can Do Attitude, Goal Setting, Planning, and Win.Draw.Learn.

Better Together

Share an example from your own life where working together resulted in a great result. Choose a situation in your life where you could ask for help but have not done so yet. What could a partner or team bring to the situation that would add value?

Always Improve

What is it that you are 'best' at? How could you improve whatever that is even more? Do you see how if you think something is as good as it can be, immediately additional progress is blocked? What in your personal or work life would you like to improve?

ABOUT THE AUTHOR

Elliott Neff is the founder and CEO of Chess4Life, which exists to help students develop life skills through the game of chess.

Elliott is a USCF (United State Chess Federation) National Master in Chess, a ranking achieved along the path to becoming the Washington State high school chess champion.

Starting with coaching his high school teammates, Elliott honed his coaching skills, now having personally trained over 10,000 students from beginners through national champions. He holds the Professional Chess Coaching Certification Level V, the highest awarded certification by the USCF.

At a pivotal moment in Elliott's life, he considered leaving the realm of competitive chess in order to focus on things that would make a positive impact in the lives of others. However, parent after parent of students whom he coached expressed how learning chess had improved their child's focus, sportsmanship, goal setting, and more. These conversations led to the realization that chess could be the vehicle by which to accomplish the impact desired.

Elliott founded Chess4Life in 2005, which now has a goal of influencing 1 million students per week with life skills through chess.

A Pawn's Journey is Elliott's first novel, inspired by stories of students. Find out more at www.ElliottNeff.com.